Praise for *Let It Be Said*

"What many of us have known for [...] through this valuable volume of reflections—Greg Funderburk is a thoughtful, faithful minister of the gospel whose wise words and winsome ways encourage others to follow more closely a God who loves and leads, especially in tumultuous times. While not a panacea, *Let It Be Said We've Borne It Well* is a well-spring for a life lived well unto God and for the good of others be it in or beyond a pandemic. This book is a gift that will help you to look for and to lean into God's glorious and mysterious future one day and one step at a time."

—Todd D. Still
Charles J. and Eleanor McLerran DeLancey Dean &
William M. Hinson Professor of Christian Scriptures
Truett Seminary, Baylor University,

"Looking for hope, encouragement, community, gift-wrapped in stories of wonder, inspiration and care? Welcome to your Happy Place! With encyclopedic knowledge, kaleidoscopic selection, and therapeutic companionship, Greg Funderburk offers us grace for our journey, peace for today and hope for tomorrow. A must read for our times!"

—J. Randall O'Brien
President Emeritus
Carson-Newman University
Author, Set Free by Forgiveness: The Way to Peace and Healing

"Greg Funderburk offers us practical wisdom we need to live well, especially in the midst of COVID-19 and its effects. The year 2020 caused tremendous disruptions and resulted in profound discouragement, yet in the midst of turbulent times Funderburk points to the God who holds the future and encourages us to live graciously and well in the light of Christ. A beautiful set of reflections to help us bear this turbulence well."

—L. Gregory Jones
Dean and Williams Distinguished Professor
Duke Divinity School

"With articulate, concise, engaging, confessional style, Greg invites us to personal reflection and living well. Integrating personal story, literature, history, technology, the arts, sciences, scripture, prayer, theology and more, he calls us to follow God amidst this tragic global pandemic. While pungent brief chapters focus on living well during COVID-19, this insightful book and its spiritual gems will inspire us to live more fully and faithfully for decades to come."

—Tim P. VanDuivendyk
Author of *The Unwanted Gift of Grief*

"Challenged in personal ways by the unrelenting difficulties, anxieties, and wrenching losses brought on by the COVID-19 pandemic, all of us have been affected by collective losses and challenges we had neither the strength, experience, nor resources to handle. In *Let It Be Said We've Borne It Well*, Greg Funderburk provides not only nuggets of rich insight, deep wisdom, and spiritual comfort to strengthen our courage but also an invitation to rise to the challenges of bearing well that for which we did not ask, but must handle.

Written in a format that allows us to take the brief chapters as offerings of grace amidst the trials, Funderburk provides keys to self-awareness, self-care, and self-giving, all of which are far more growth-producing than the temptations of self-pity. Integrating the ageless truths in these chapters into our beliefs and values and into our daily lives holds the opportunity to come through this pandemic and other trials able to say, 'Not only did I bear this well, but I am even stronger, more resilient, and more loving than I was.'

Funderburk does this in ways that assure us that while we may not bear the COVID trials perfectly, we can bear them well. And that is grace."

—Jeanie Miley
Speaker, retreat leader, and author of
Sitting Strong: Wrestling with the Ornery God
and *Practicing Resurrection: Radical Hope in Difficult Times*

LET IT BE SAID WE'VE BORNE IT WELL

FOLLOWING GOD IN THE TIME OF COVID-19

GREGORY FUNDERBURK

Smyth & Helwys Publishing, Inc.
6316 Peake Road
Macon, Georgia 31210-3960
1-800-747-3016

©2021 by Gregory Funderburk
All rights reserved.

Library of Congress Cataloging-in-Publication Data

Names: Funderburk, Gregory, 1965- author.
Title: Let it be said we've borne it well : following God in the time of
    COVID-19 / by Gregory Funderburk.
Description: Macon, GA : Smyth & Helwys, 2021. | Includes bibliographical
    references.
Identifiers: LCCN 2020055467 (print) | LCCN 2020055468 (ebook) | ISBN
    9781641732956 (paperback) | ISBN 9781641732963 (ebook)
Subjects: LCSH: Suffering--Religious aspects--Christianity. | Faith. |
    COVID-19 (Disease)--Religious aspects--Christianity. |
    Epidemics--Religious aspects--Christianity.
Classification: LCC BV4909 .F86 2021 (print) | LCC BV4909 (ebook) | DDC
    248.86/1962414--dc23
LC record available at https://lccn.loc.gov/2020055467
LC ebook record available at https://lccn.loc.gov/2020055468

Disclaimer of Liability: With respect to statements of opinion or fact available in
this work of nonfiction, Smyth & Helwys Publishing Inc. nor any of its employees,
makes any warranty, express or implied, or assumes any legal liability or responsibility
for the accuracy or completeness of any information disclosed, or represents that its
use would not infringe privately-owned rights.

To my uncle,
Larry Funderburk,
a splendid mentor in all respects.

ACKNOWLEDGMENTS

This project began as the COVID-19 pandemic descended upon us in March 2020. I began to write weekly essays to encourage the congregation that I serve as a pastor. As the weeks wore on, the thought experiment that generated the title of this book became a tentpole around which I continued to write. In this regard, since the congregation at South Main Baptist Church in Houston was both my original audience and the group of people who gave me an opportunity to serve as a minister, I wish to thank the church's members and my friends on staff: Steve Wells, Carey Cannon, Susan Moore, Brad Jernberg, Dolores Rader, and Matt Walton. A measure of immense gratitude also goes to my wife, Kelly, who helped me with ideas, subject matter, and clarity with respect to this effort, as well as to my kids, Hank and Charlie, who in some uncanny way seem to direct me toward eternal lessons I need to learn. I also wish to thank Keith Gammons, Leslie Andres, Holly Bean, and Dave Jones at Smyth & Helwys for their guidance and support in publishing this work.

CONTENTS

LET IT BE SAID WE'VE BORNE IT WELL

I've not only been thinking about the uncertainty of the future; I've also been trying to envision a *future version* of my family and myself and then asking God to take me there. *The book in your hands is about this very thing.* Picture a future version of your community and family that's closer and kinder than it is now because we've all lived through a global pandemic together. Think about a future version of yourself who, through suffering, has become more aligned with the themes of Christ's life as expressed in the Sermon on the Mount. Perhaps even consider a future version of your church that's more relevant to our changing world and our communities through the challenges we've all endured and continue to endure together.

At some point in the future, when this time in our history is considered, as for me, my family, my church, and my community, I want it to be said that *we've borne it well*. As I ponder how to get to that place, I picture a path ahead illuminated by the blessings of *self-awareness, self-care,* and *self-giving.* While this might seem like a lot of "selfs," I don't mean it in a self-centered or self-aggrandizing way. Rather, it's the opposite—I want to recognize and want to encourage others to recognize that our lives are a windfall. We've done nothing to deserve them, and they are gifts to be crafted, curated, and offered back to God. With that in mind, let's look at each of these "self" notions more expansively.

SELF-AWARENESS

As I write this, we remain in a hard season, and whether you know it or not, whether you name it or not, whether you stop to feel it or not, you're grieving right now. In one way or another, we're all feeling a loss of a measure of the life we thought we were going to have and are trying to recapture. Some of our social fabric has unraveled around this moment in time due to isolation and abridgment of community, and if we're not self-aware about it—if we fail to name the losses we've experienced or anticipate experiencing—we may shift our negative feelings around this grief onto the wrong thing or, most often, onto a person close to us. The truth is that an event, person, or comment that we often think of as the last straw is usually not the actual thing that's made us impatient, resentful, or angry. We're mad at this season, these losses, this moment in time. Identifying, naming aloud, and meditating on what's producing the anxiety, fear, sorrow, contempt, and anger inside us is the only way to keep our real frustrations from coming out in the wrong way or onto the wrong person. This is grief. It's exhausting. Attend to it. *I hope this book helps you do this.*

SELF-CARE

There's a reason Jesus often went off to be by himself in the midst of the profound teaching and crucial healing work of his ministry. Like him, we need sleep. We need quiet. We need sunshine. We need healthy food, exercise, and routines. We need time to think. We need Sabbath. We need peace of mind. We need plans and reliable expectations. We need creative input. All of these have been hard to come by in a pandemic—or any crisis—and thus we need a higher level of intentionality if we're to experience them as fuel.

As you care for yourself, you certainly know what you need more than anyone. Whatever that is, move it up in the priority list. This book—full of stories and references not only to the sacred but also to the mundane (and even the profane at times)—is meant to provide some imaginative prompts and ideas that encourage you to do the work of *reframing and refueling.* In remarkable ways, music, literature, poetry, film, nature, friendship, sports, and pop culture provide lines for God to broadcast to us, reach us through our humanity, and fill and refill our souls. All of this is especially needed now. If you need permission, an invitation, some guidance, a strong hand of instruction, or an outright command to take the time to care for yourself, *here it is.*

SELF-GIVING

Finally, when the walls close in on us both physically and emotionally, our vision narrows and we tend to see things only from our own point of view. When you feel yourself being edged into this corner, intentionally flip the script and volunteer to do something for another person. This is something that reliably expands our vision, air-lifting us out of the self-absorption zone. And I hasten to add that if you're caring for kids or an elderly parent, serving your community, or looking out for someone who is vulnerable right now, take a deep breath and realize that work, which may seem routine or "just part of your job," is the very thing on which true religion is based.

God bless you. This book endeavors to point you toward such realizations and opportunities in order to help reframe your experience into a larger context that values gratitude, humility, and the recognition of blessing and beauty all around us, as well as the grace offered to us each day.

My prayer for all of us, the one that's deeply enmeshed throughout this work, is that we will begin to form in our minds and hearts an image of the future that God desires for us and for the world. As you read along, whether all at once or day by day, ask God to take you there—to illumine the path ahead as we continue to navigate through this difficult time, this troubled season, together.

And let it be said we've borne it well.

SELF-AWARENESS

"All of humanity's problems stem from man's inability to sit quietly in a room alone." —Blaise Pascal (from *Pensées: The Provincial Letters* [Section 2, "The Misery of Man without God," Letter 139])

CHAPTER 1

"WHAT YOU DON'T KNOW YOU CAN FEEL IT SOMEHOW"

Every time I doubt God's presence in my life, I remember this story: My sister Susan, who lives in Los Angeles, was about to catch a plane to Houston to attend my ordination service when she texted me this: *I think Bono is on my flight.*

Bono is the lead singer of the Irish band U2. As a Christian, he sees his celebrity as currency to use for causes like debt relief and feeding the hungry. A charismatic front man of a musical act that's packed arenas for more than four decades, he's one of the most famous people in the world. Speaking at the National Prayer Breakfast a few years ago, Bono crafted a beautiful gospel message around Matthew 25, quoting what he's said on a number of occasions is his favorite Scripture passage: "Inasmuch as you've done it unto the least of these my brethren, you have done it unto me" (v. 40; based on KJV).

Bono is short with reddish-brown hair, has a thick Irish accent, and is almost invariably wearing trademark rock star sunglasses, usually an outrageously hued pink or purple. He's also a millionaire many times over. So I texted my sister back.

> Greg: Aren't you on Southwest Airlines?
> Susan: Yes. I'm in Boarding Group B. Bono's in Group A.
> Greg: It's not Bono.
> Susan: It's Bono.
> Greg: Get me his autograph.

A few hours later I got another text—a video from the plane. In it, my sister and Bono are talking like old chums. When he got up to go to the bathroom, she apparently followed him, cornered him when he came out, and began filming their interaction (apparently with his permission). In the video, they banter a bit, and then this happens:

Bono *(strong Irish accent)*: What's your brother's name again?

Susan: Greg.

Bono *(to camera)*: Greg, congratulations on your ordination. God be with you wherever you go. And remember, "As you've done it unto the least of these, my brother, you have done it unto me." God bless you.

I immediately sent the video to my youngest sister, Laura, who lives in Washington. She expressed skepticism. She watched the video and texted back.

Laura: Why would Bono be going to Houston on Southwest? Doesn't make sense. Really think it was him?

Greg: Looks like Bono. Sounds like Bono. Moves like Bono. Even quoted Bono's favorite verse. *It's Bono.*

Laura: I have my doubts.

We live in a world doused in skepticism, and, especially now, we live in a season of doubt. Small doubts like *Was that really Bono?* And also big doubts like *Is this going to get better? Where's God in all this?*

When it comes down to it, the question is not if we will doubt. God knows we will doubt. The real question is how God wants us to deal with doubt. Here's what Jesus said to the disciple we know as "Doubting Thomas": "Because you have seen me and at present have me within your range of vision, you have believed, with the result that you are in a state of belief. But spiritually prosperous are those who, not having seen, yet believe" (John 20: 29, Kenneth Wuest's Expanded Greek Translation).

Christ doesn't say there's joy in doubt, but he does say there's a kind of joy in *transcending* doubt, and the Gospel of John gives us a hint on how we might do this. It's peculiarly compelling, isn't it, that each post-Resurrection appearance Jesus makes in John's Gospel focuses on a different human sense?

At the tomb, Mary Magdalene recognizes the resurrected Jesus not by sight—she thinks he's the gardener when she first lays eyes on him—but by his *voice* when he calls her name. She recognizes him by *sound.* When the resurrected Jesus first appears to the disciples in the upper room, the Scripture says they believe when they *see* him. The recognition is focused on their sense of *sight.* Then, after Peter has denied Jesus near a charcoal fire at night, a few days later the risen Christ appears to him, and they share breakfast over another charcoal fire. That is to say, the same scent that infused Peter's earlier betrayal now perfumes the very grace and mercy Jesus offers him. The *scent* is central to the story. Finally, Thomas (who was not present at the earlier appearances), comes to believe when he lays his hands on and in Christ's wounds. "My Lord," he confesses, "and my God." The sense of *touch* is what dispels his doubts.

John is telling us that we discover the resurrected Jesus with *all* of our human senses—in the things we hear with our ears, the things we see with our eyes, the scents we smell with our noses, and the things we touch with our hands. It's also interesting that, even now, the church remembers the crucified and risen Christ just as he instructed, by using our sense of taste in sharing Communion, the Eucharist.

As we've worked our way through a brutal calendar of months and prepare for continued trials ahead, consider this: when you experience glimpses, those fleeting occasions that feel like *God-in-the-present-moment* in a way that approaches certainty and fortifies your faith with joy, whether by ear, eyes, nose, touch, or taste, call it out as Thomas did. Let these impressionistic moments address your doubts. In the sound of breaking waves, the soaring music of Mozart, or even the rock and roll of U2, say it: "My Lord and my God." In the perfect angle of sunlight through the clouds in the late afternoon, call it out again. In the smell of fresh oranges: "My Lord and my God." In the moment your child grabs your hand: "My Lord and my God." In the taste of honey and toasted bread: "My Lord and my God."

To put it another way, as my "good friend" Bono sings in one of his most famous songs, "Beautiful Day": "What you don't know you can feel it somehow."

> God, in the moments when I feel, through my senses, the beautiful things I believe but may not completely know, may I receive and then attend the promised blessing made to those who may doubt but neverthe-less believe. Amen.

CHAPTER 2

ENDURANCE

"On Friday night in the Cumberland Mountains of east Tennessee, 28 men and seven women lie in tents half-asleep anticipating the sound of a conch shell echoing through the Big Cove Campgrounds." That's how Dave Seminara begins his 2013 *New York Times* story about the Barkley Marathon, a 100-mile footrace through the wilderness of Tennessee's Frozen Head State Park. Long before the conch sounds, the racers, seeking to test themselves against nature and one another, are already survivors of sorts. The "Barkley," as it is known, is almost as tough to enter as it is to compete in. "You've got to do some real ninja thinking just to get in," one contestant said.[1]

There's no website explaining how to enter and no set race date. The first step is to figure out where and when to send a required essay on why one should be allowed to compete, pay the peculiar $1.60 entry fee, and take an exam with curious questions like "What's the most important vegetable group?" If you do get in, the race organizer, a man compellingly named Lazarus Lake, sends you a condolence letter, urging you to rethink your decision.

You have to be a tremendous athlete to take on the Barkley, but you also need to be a gifted route-finder. There's a rudimentary map posted at the start, but the runners have to copy it down themselves. Once the conch sounds, they all launch into the mountains facing sleet and freezing temperatures along the highest ridges and then blistering heat in the valleys below. "The course is the primary villain," a veteran racer said. The terrain, with multiple ascents and descents, is equivalent to climbing Mount Everest twice, all within the race's sixty-hour time limit that forces competitors to rush through heavy thorns and brambles with little or no sleep. In addition, throughout the race, Lake taunts the competitors, playing taps on an old bugle whenever a racer succumbs to the course's brutality and drops out.

To confirm that no one cheats, Lake's co-organizer, known only as Raw Dog, hides ten books with titles like *Heart of Darkness* and *Doomed* at points along the course, requiring runners to rip out the page of the book that matches their race number. There are no comfort stations, no GPS devices, and no cellphones allowed. For the first ten years of the race, no one finished. Then one person did, and then six years passed before the next one did. All told, only eighteen people, less than 2 percent of the nearly eight hundred ultra-runners, have ever completed the race. "All the other big races are set up for you to succeed. The Barkley's set up for you to fail. The clock doesn't stop," Lake says, "and it's not going to go as planned."

Does any of this sound familiar? Is this what your life sometimes feels like these days? Do you feel like you're in a race over perilous unmarked territory with hopeless instructions, an array of mostly unknown forces aligned against you? We've been in the midst of a savagely uncooperative season. And there will be other seasons like it. So it's important to ask, what do you do when you don't know the terrain ahead, how long the race might be, or even if you're still on the course?

St. Paul, in all his prolific epistle-writing, used a racing metaphor once or twice. Once he even set out a rough map for us. Suffering, he told his Roman friends, produces perseverance; perseverance, character; and character, hope (Rom 5:3-4). When we suffer, we want hope to follow on quick, but we have to stay to the route, station to station. Suffering doesn't lead *immediately* to hope but first to perseverance, and then it's perseverance—the experiential grit that cuts the grooves into our lives like lines in the face of an old actor playing a consequential part—that leads to character. The hope that Scripture promises *then* emerges from the strength and earned confidence that character bestows. *Station to station. Step by step. You've got to follow the map.*

"We're made to endure challenges," Lazarus Lake says. "The real joy's seeing people who find something in themselves that they didn't know was there."

We're all doing something arduous right now in this present orbit around the sun, but, as another one of the Barkley racers said in what seems like his own translation of Romans,

> When you go through something like this, you can say you've struggled. You've overcome. You've gotten through. Then you're more confident. You not only enjoy your life more, you feel like you can do things. You can take on other challenges you wouldn't otherwise try. You'll get to points that you wouldn't have otherwise reached.

Stay on course.

God, when the trail seems to disappear and the map seems confusing, grant me strength to endure and the faith to trust the sequence: suffering leads to perseverance, perseverance to character, character to hope. Amen.

CHAPTER 3

NOW

The neuroscientists have reported in. They estimate that our brains consider *now* to be about three seconds long, and *now* is always vanishing into thin air right before us. That is to say, *now* is a slippery little sucker, a moving target. There it goes again. And again. And again.

Daniel Kahneman is a psychology professor at Princeton. He won the 2002 Nobel Prize in Economics and wrote the bestseller *Thinking, Fast and Slow*. He tells us,

> There are about 20,000 of these three second moments in a 16-hour day. This is what life consists of, a sequence of moments. Each moment is actually very rich in experience. If you stop someone and ask—"What's happening to you right *now*?"—a great deal is happening. There's a mental content, there's a physical state, there's a mood, there might be emotion. Many things are happening.[1]

The word *mindfulness* is everywhere these days. It means so many things to so many different people. I know it might have some baggage; maybe it strikes you as a fuzzy new age hocus-pocus concept. You might even want to roll your eyes when you hear it. Let me explain in a sentence what it means to me: mindfulness slows *now* down. It's taking some deep breaths, bringing your mind to a crawl, and just being open and still for a bit. It lengthens the concept of *now* and reins in its elusive nature.

Our days have become blurry, running into one another without the routines and old habits of coming in and going out, the familiar markers of normal work and school, labor and Sabbath, weekdays and weekends. The iPhone had already taken a wrecking ball to mindfulness, but as we've braved quasi-quarantine and a season of social isolation, this experience has accelerated the erosion of the boundary between the imperative of getting stuff done and the living of all the other moments in our lives.

In this context, mindfulness, the idea of stopping and clearing your consciousness every so often, is more important than ever. It's a way to listen to the Divine speaking, maybe not in words, but so that we can tune into God's constant broadcast into the silence of our minds, if indeed we can endeavor to silence them for a time. It's a way of resetting our posture, which seems to always be leaning forward and ahead into the next moment, even when we're happy. This proclivity, which expresses perhaps the core human dysfunction of our time, leads us into a state where we hardly enjoy even the good things that come to us, instead continually moving the goal-posts out ahead. Mindfulness pushes back against this tendency. It tells us we can't *become* happy; we can only *be* happy. This is all to say that if we want to live the joyous life that God offers us, we can't keep telling ourselves a story about what set of circumstances must happen in the future in order for us to *become* happy and to feel joyful.

Here's an alternative idea: when something good happens, stop and be mindful of how you feel in it as it's occurring. Enjoy it. You might even want to snap a picture of it. Not a real one—we have enough of those—but one just for your mind. Lift up your hands to your eyes and click. Feel the shutter open and close. It slows you down and tells your heart, "keep this." *Grant the present moment sufficient attention so as to be captivated by it.*

> God, I know I have a real bias toward movement and the future and against stillness and the present. You've given me 20,000 *nows* today. Help me to mine at least a few of them more deeply, to be present within them, to slow the fleeting sense of them, to bring some mindfulness to these bountiful and miraculous gifts, asking not "*What else do I have to do or think or worry about?*" but "*What does it feel like in this moment to be here with my family, my friends, my neighbors, or only You?*" Amen.

CHAPTER 4

PERFECTLY IMPERFECT

There's a beautiful section in David McCullough's biography of John Adams in which he describes the prolific letter-writing of Adams's gifted wife, Abigail. An avid reader, she quoted poetry in most of what she wrote. "Every letter had a line or two of poetry in it," McCullough said later in talks he presented about his book. He pointed out that small errors appeared in her quotations, revealing to McCullough not that she was an imprecise writer but rather that she was recalling these poetic lines by heart. Her imperfections revealed to him a distinct beauty of mind as well as a heart freighted with deep and poignant wisdom.[1]

In a recent article in *Psychology Today*, a cultural psychologist named Marianna Pogosyan offered insight on this same theme of imperfection and beauty:

> Centuries back, in the height of the Japanese autumn, in one of Kyoto's majestic gardens . . . a young man trimmed the hedges, raked the gravel, picked the dried leaves from the stones, cleared the moss path of twigs. The garden looked immaculate: not a blade of grass out of place. His master inspected the garden quietly. Then, he reached up to a branch of a maple tree and shook it, watching the auburn leaves fall with haphazard grace on tidied earth. There it was now, the magic of imperfection.[2]

The concept of *wabi-sabi* is characteristic of the Japanese idea of beauty—one in which minor imperfections create a hint of melancholy and a spiritual sense of incompleteness and longing that, as they direct the eye, also lead the soul toward a deeper comprehension of the beauty at hand.

This theme appears in music as well. In his book *How Music Works*, musician David Byrne, best known as the singer for the band Talking Heads, explains how a singer can reliably import additional beauty and emotional octane into a performance simply by shifting a sung note off the rhythm of the song just a little.

> A good singer will often use the "grid" of the rhythm as something to play with—never landing exactly on the beat, but pushing and pulling

around and against it . . . . When Willie Nelson or George Jones sing way off a beat, it somehow increases the sense that they're telling you a story, conveying it to you, one person to another.[3]

Consider the flawed beauty of some of our most iconic movie stars, the asymmetry of some of the most remarkable architecture, and the fact that some of the best comedy arises when an actor flubs his lines and another ad-libs into the scene. Once a grasshopper got stuck to the canvas as Vincent Van Gogh painted a scene in the woods, yet his *Olive Trees* painting is one of the most valuable and beautiful pieces at the Nelson-Atkins Museum in Kansas City. "Even happiness," Pogosyan writes, "at close inspection, has its wrinkles and rough edges. But there is also a relief. A release from the hostage of perfection."[4]

Despite sensing that all this is true, we still constantly strive for perfection. I'm doing it right now as I proofread these words searching for typos (or is it typo's?). It's exhausting, isolating, and, perhaps most important, it's counter to an easily detected thread that runs through Scripture.

Look at the lineage of Jesus that reaches back to the Old Testament. Matthew opens his Gospel with this lineage. It is imperfection personified. Jacob, not an ideal role model, appears early on. Then Judah and Tamar—that's embarrassing, to put it mildly. Odd judges, bad kings, and even the heroes have issues and some real rough edges. Don't look too closely at Rahab's résumé or Ruth's birthplace. Having women in an ancient Jewish genealogy is remarkable enough, and then finally there are David and Bathsheba. Next, take the life of Jesus himself—*that's one unusually messy origin story.* There are peculiar detours with tax collectors and lots of other sinners. His opponents were always on him for the company he kept. He had an odd assortment of stumbling colleagues and a pretty scandalous second-to-last chapter of his life, if you hadn't noticed. Even post-resurrection, Jesus is mistaken for a gardener.

There's something resonant and magnetic in the unsanitized version, though, and this fact alone implies that *when we draw the curtains on the real and most authentic parts of our own lives, we're liable to miss out on some of the most crucial things God has for us.* There's real beauty, power, and poignancy in the imperfect and even the broken. It's often in these afflicted moments that we make the most touching connections that somehow bless God and each other most. Relax a little and resolve to embrace them. And if this isn't the perfect ending to this chapter, it's close enough.

God, may I strive not for an idolatrous perfection that turns me inward but strive to turn outward, *as I am*—hands open and eyes open to the world's imperfect beauty, which leaves still more room for grace. Amen.

CHAPTER 5

REROUTED

At 10:00 in the morning on a day early in June 1998, Trisha McFarlane, age nine, was wearing her blue Boston Red Sox batting practice jersey and playing with her doll, Mona, in the backseat of her mother's Dodge Caravan. By 10:30, she was lost in the woods. By 11:00, she was trying not to be terrified, trying not to think, *"This is serious."* Trying not to think how sometimes people who get lost in the woods get hurt. How sometimes they die.

Trisha had stepped off the hiking trail when nature called. She had walked down a small slope for some privacy, and then a sense of modesty pushed her little farther, then a little farther. When she was done, she made the biggest mistake of her life—she went forward instead of back-tracking. Trisha walked along for about ten minutes or so, then stopped. And now, in that tense place between her chest and her stomach, where all the body's wires come together in a clump, she felt the first *minnow-y* flutter of disquiet. Tears formed in the corners of her eyes, and she blinked them back savagely. If she started to cry, she wouldn't be able to tell herself she wasn't frightened. If she started to cry, anything could happen.

That's how author Stephen King begins the action of his novel, *The Girl Who Loved Tom Gordon.*[1] King nails the feeling that emerges in us when we first realize we're lost. *Lost.* Just the word itself can cause that little flutter.

Fortunately, with the miracles of GPS technology, it's getting harder and harder to get lost. Soon, perhaps we'll be able to stick tiny little GPS devices on everything we own, and we'll never lose anything again. If I'd only had some of this technology when I was growing up. I kept some of my best baseball cards in plastic sheets in a nice binder, and I turned my parents' house upside down several times over looking for it. But now it's gone. *Lost.* What if I had some sort of advanced technology so I could track down my old Willie Mays cards, Hank Aaron, Roberto Clemente—what a thrill it would be to find such long-lost treasures.

Movie director Ang Lee refers to the emotional effect of capturing that moment of being lost and then suddenly being found, that moment of rediscovery of a long-lost love or a lost treasure, that moment of reunion, that moment the lost hero returns as "the juice." Lee says, "Whatever I bring into my films, I am forever trying to update and recapture that feeling. I call it juice—the juice of the film—the thing that moves people, the thing that is untranslatable by words."[2] It is the switch when the desperation of being lost gives way to the sheer jubilation of being found.

This beautiful *lost then found* language is exactly what Jesus uses to explain what we are like and what God is like. Lost and found stories resonate with us because no matter how far technology advances, no matter how many GPS dots we stick onto things, stories about what is lost and then found will always capture us because they represent something at the core of the human condition. And regardless of advancements in technology, there will never be a clever enough app that can eliminate the pain of losing a job or losing our savings due to a desperate miscalculated gamble. There's no GPS system to prevent that *minnow-y* feeling between our chest and stomach when we're told our spouse's medical treatment is no longer working, or that we're losing our memory and soon we're going to lose ourselves. And there's no pleasant-sounding voice to call up on our smartphones when what we thought wasn't a big deal has now become an addiction that's taking us further and further away from ourselves every day. There's no innovation to download when we've betrayed someone or something or God and we can't take it back. We can't simply type an address in our car's navigational system and banish that feeling of dislocation and self-doubt so we can get back home. We don't have such technology, *but we do have a story*—a parable told by Jesus and captured in Luke's Gospel—about being lost.

We best remember the Pharisees for their legalism and hypocrisy, their constant opposition to Jesus, and their persecution of early Christians, and this story about being lost then found begins with them grumbling in a way that's typical of them: "This fellow, this Jesus," they complain, "is giving sinners access to himself, giving them his companionship, even eating with them." Jesus quickly picks up on their attitude, and, knowing that matters often go poorly when you start with harsh truth-telling about how your audience is going the wrong way, he launches into a story. It's almost like he sees them take a wrong turn on the road and *reroutes* them in a way that's not unlike the voice in our smartphone rerouting us when we get off track.

"If you have a hundred sheep and lose one of them, of course," Jesus says to his listeners in Luke 15:4, "you go after the lost one, right?" *It's a great question.* One that makes you think. One way of looking at it would be to say, "Well, no." That doesn't sound like a good idea at all. It sounds like a poor utilization of resources. In any reasonable risk-reward analysis, it honestly sounds pretty foolish. Economically, the equation doesn't add up.

We don't do this, do we? Leave ninety-nine for the one?

Is this what God is like?

As Jesus reroutes his listeners, that's what he's telling them . . . *and us.* Yes, this is the way God thinks about us.

What if we could update this parable and show ourselves that perhaps we *do* have this instinct too? Wouldn't it make sense that if we have it, it's because God has it and gave it to us?

In the early morning hours of Wednesday, October 14, 1987, an eighteen-month-old toddler named Jessica McClure removed a flower pot that covered a hole in her aunt's backyard in Midland, Texas, and she fell through an eight-inch-wide opening into an abandoned well shaft. Bobby Jo Hall was a thirty-two-year-old Midland police officer at the time.

"I was the first officer at the scene," Hall said. "I arrived at the same time as the paramedics. The mother met us at the front door of the house. . . . She said, 'I can't let my baby die. . . .' I went over and looked down the hole, but I couldn't see anything. I called the baby's name three or four times and didn't hear anything. Finally I got a cry in response. We didn't know how deep she was until we lowered a tape hooked to a flashlight into the hole."[3]

Jessica was twenty-two feet under the ground.

"It was wild. We tore down fences; we tore down clotheslines—all kinds of things to get that equipment in. The first thing we tried was a backhoe the city brought over. It dug down two or three feet and then hit rock. . . . I was there twenty-two hours," Hall remembered.

"When we weren't calling words of encouragement," Detective Andy Glasscock recalled, "we'd tell her to sing for us. I'll never forget her singing 'Winnie-the-Pooh.' We'd say, 'How does a kitten go?' And she'd respond to us."[4]

David Lilly worked for MSHA, the United States Mine and Safety Health Administration, in 1987. He arrived the second day. By Thursday evening, he said they'd already sunk a parallel shaft about twenty-nine feet into the ground through a hole thirty inches wide and had started to drill a horizontal drift toward the well. It was bringing them to the spot where Jessica was, but they would've broken the well right into her. "I changed the angle of the horizontal drift," Lilly said, "so it would break through two feet below her . . . . Then we would take down a 45-pound jackhammer, also with a tungsten bit, and hold it there to knock out the rock. We were going at about an inch an hour. . . . But I've never seen more dedicated people."

In Midland, Texas, the equation had changed. What everyone was doing for the next fifty-eight hours could wait. They'd all been rerouted to save a single little girl, lost.

A poet named Lucy Brock-Broido wrote a long and emotional poem called "Jessica from the Well." Here are some powerful excerpts. It's from little Jessica's point of view, the point of view of someone lost and yearning to be found.

> This is what it was like: the morning
> pale all above me, a patch of sky . . .
> I am on my knees at first, a Jessica
> in prayer. I pray against the rose
> caliche, the hardpan rock . . . .
>
> I am the only one alive.
>
> By dusk, I am running out
> of ways to warm myself.
> . . . .
>
> By midnight, I can hear my own heart thump
> against the well . . . .
>
> Big gangly weeping gamey men, Sweethearts &
> Insomniacs,
> keep prodding me *to sing*.
> And I sing.
>
> . . . *How does a kitten go?*
> And I go like a kitten goes . . . .
>
> Bring me back
> alive. It was so simple to come down. . . .[5]

Was there anyone who begrudged, Pharisee-like, the thousands of hours expended and the hundreds of thousands of dollars spent on the equipment used to rescue a little girl lost? *Maybe there was, but they don't know what God is like, and they don't acknowledge what we can be like—for in this true story we whispered what God is like.* It's God's very nature to give us the continual experience of being found against the world's continuous story of being lost.

As soon as I miss a turn or go off track with my GPS, I'm always amazed not only how fast the voice comes on to tell me it's rerouting but that it's happening at all—it keeps rerouting and rerouting as long as I'm lost. And just like that, every time we go off the path, God sees the bigger picture, God sees our location, God sees our situation and our destination. And God begins plotting a new way back. Listen, and proceed to the route.

> God, in this strange time of lostness, reroute us and reroute us so that we may be found again and again. Amen.

CHAPTER 6

WEAR IT

Like many churches, ours sets aside resources to help folks in need in our community. Tom Williams, the most senior minister on staff when I started, showed me how our church handled this ministry. He had such a graceful way of speaking with those who came in need, often off the streets, but he also had a knack for asking just the right questions to find out if our church could truly help the person with respect to the need.

One of the first benevolence requests I was asked to handle on my own involved a young man who was asking for a bus ticket to Tampa. Following what I'd seen Tom do, I asked the man why he wanted to go to Florida, and he replied that this was where he was from, that Florida was his home. Out of a sense of due diligence, I asked a few more questions, but as I did, my voice must have slipped into the tone it used to take when I practiced law, cross-examining witnesses. "Now, sir," I asked, "do you plan on staying in Florida? Do have family in Florida? *Sir, just how committed are you to the state of Florida?*"

The man answered my rapid-fire inquiries until he got to the last one, about his commitment to the Sunshine State. Then he looked me right in the eye as if he'd been waiting his whole life to answer this one, and he lifted up his shirt to reveal—emblazoned all the way across his chest—a giant tattoo in the shape of the state of *Florida*.

I got him the ticket.

This story comes to mind when, in unsteady times like this, I consider what I'm doing and who I am. Am I as committed to my God-given identity as that Floridian was to his? In the book of Colossians, Paul encourages us to see ourselves as God sees us—*holy, chosen, and beloved* (3:12). Paul urges us to embrace this identity even if we don't always feel like the words completely fit.

One of the casualties of the pandemic has been the last baseball season. Teams played a number of games, but there were anomalies: seven-inning doubleheaders, a universal designated hitter, and, in extra innings, a runner who started the inning on second base. With it being a weird season, I suppose you can change some of the rules in baseball, but it's a little tougher to change the unwritten rules. And in baseball, there are lots of unwritten rules. There's this one: if you're hit by a pitch, you're not to give the pitcher the satisfaction of seeing that it hurt you. You're just to run down to first base like it was nothing.

A couple of summers ago, my son Charlie was playing in a high school game, and sure enough the pitcher dotted him with an errant high-velocity pitch right to his midsection, and you could tell it hurt. Charlie just dropped his bat and took his base like it was nothing. And as he ran down the baseline, his buddies in the dugout yelled, "That's the way, Charlie, wear it!"

If Charlie can wear a fastball to the ribs, as uncomfortable as that must have been, then perhaps we can try on these words and wear them as well. Let's start with *chosen*. In George Wiegel's superb biography of Pope John Paul II titled *Witness to Hope*, he wrote about the Christian idea of chosen-ness.[1] Being chosen involves strange detours, some long and twisting roads, the unexpected, and sometimes even the tragic, all of which lead to an understanding that, in the final analysis, you're simply not in charge of your own life. As Christ followers, we're chosen in the sense that we're called, counterculturally, to be the ones who put others before ourselves, to love our enemies, and to cross the road *Good Samaritan-like* when we see others in need. This often puts us on a peculiar path, or at least it should. What God knows and we often forget is that this strange journey of chosen-ness puts us on the elusive path on which true human flourishing is found. *You're chosen for this sort of life, so put it on—wear it.*

Next, Paul calls us to be *holy*. Last year, I took a genetic test. It turns out I'm 72 percent British/Irish, 13 percent Northwestern European, 11 percent French/German, 2 percent Scandinavian, 1 percent Iberian, and 1 percent Finnish. I also learned that I'm unlikely to be able to sing on pitch and am genetically inclined to have a slight aversion to cilantro. We can identify ourselves in all sorts of ways—by our heritage, by our gender, by the roles we take on, by our appearance, by our achievements, by our economic status, by our failures, and even by our sins. But God is intent on getting under all of that, insisting first and foremost that we identify ourselves not by anything we've done or failed to do but by what God has done for us *in Christ*. That is, we're to look in the mirror every morning and, as a matter of faithfulness, gratitude, obedience, and memory, to define ourselves as God does. In God's own holy image. *In Christ.* That is to say, when God thinks of us, God sees us but also sees Christ's work, and therefore Christ's reflection, in us. So again, lean into this: *Holy. Put it on. Wear it.*

Beloved is not a word we hear a lot anymore. Google Ngram is an online search engine that charts the frequency of use of any given word in virtually any written and published source—newspapers, books, and publications printed between 1500 and the present. You can see how often a word has been used and track how certain words go in and out of favor over time. While absolutely rocking it in the 1700s and 1800s, the word *beloved* has lost serious market share in the last century or so. It's been relegated mostly to sonnets and cemetery headstones. But we need to bring it back because God uses it for us. And what it means is not just that God loves us but also that God calls us to *beloved-ness*, to congregate with one another, meeting with frequency, bonding over making and listening to music with one another and doing shared tasks together in a way that, again, becomes a part of our identity. *Beloved-ness* is not something that is meant to be exclusionary, designed to set us ahead of everyone else, but rather it's to be a part of our identity, a garment to be worn that reminds us and summons us to expand the boundaries and definition of "neighbor," calling us toward and along a selfless path on which the spell of this world is broken. *Beloved. Put it on. Wear it.*

> God, help me to put on this identity, to wear it—*chosen, holy, and beloved.* Emblazon it indelibly across my life as I forge ahead. Amen.

CHAPTER 7

MISSING NOTHING

When Johann Sebastian Bach died in 1750, he wasn't thought of as an especially brilliant composer, and within a few years of his death, he and his music were largely forgotten. But in 1823, seventy-three years after his death, a German woman named Bella Salomon presented a birthday gift to her fifteen-year-old grandson, Felix. The gift was a manuscript score of Bach's *St. Matthew's Passion*, which put to music the story of the death, crucifixion, and resurrection of Christ. Although essentially unknown at that time, the music so captivated young Felix that he dreamt grandly of its performance.

It took Felix Mendelssohn the next five years of his young life to arrange, organize, and prepare the Passion to be performed at Berlin's *Singakademie* on March 11, 1829. To say it was well received would be an understatement. It led not only to a revival but to a complete reevaluation of Bach's works, first in Germany and then in Europe, until Bach's significance was recognized not just as genius but as virtually unparalleled in history the world over. Even now, some of our greatest musicians like the cellist Yo-Yo Ma rightly ask, what power did Bach possess that, even after 300 years, his music continues to help us through troubled times?

I want to suggest an answer—an answer that may help us navigate not just this challenging season but any subsequent period of trial and difficulty ahead. For as the world rediscovered Bach, it also saw that before writing even a single note of a new composition, at the top of the first page Bach would first write the letters "JJ," which stood for *Jesu Juva*, Latin for "Jesus, help." The music would then begin to pour from his soul until, at the end of each composition, he'd write at the bottom of the score the letters "SDG," *Soli Deo Gloria*, Latin for "Glory to God alone."

What if we prayed these two phrases or even wrote them down at the beginning and end of every day? What if we asked for Christ's help every morning and then sanctified the day's work to God's glory every evening as we close our eyes? And what if, between these two moments of devotion, we asked God for the eyes, the ears, and the heart to see, hear, and feel what genius, what comfort, and what beauty we might be missing all around us? Like Bach's music before Mendelssohn had rediscovered it, what richness might we be missing simply because we're not paying close enough attention, not looking the right way, or have simply forgotten it?

God is all around us, broadcasting wisdom, solace, grace, and love in all the ways an invisible God can. Through open lines of prayer. Through the guidance of conscience. By tapping us on the shoulder with the close connections of family and friendship. With the revelation of all sorts of Scripture—stories, songs, poetry, history. God is in the sonic architecture of music, in the colors of the rolling sea, and in the ripples of wispy clouds at dawn. In the bonding of teammates contending fairly on the field of sport. In the contours of soaring buildings. In the color and genius of art and artists. In the drama of film. In the lessons of literature. In the wholesome feeling we get when we cross the street and serve those in need. In the sacred. In the mundane. In the profane.

The Killers are a terrific rock band out of Fabulous Las Vegas. Brandon Flowers, the group's compelling lead singer, a Mormon, grew up in Utah before moving to Vegas and, with some other gifted musicians, started the group. His faith emerges with brilliant regularity in his music. He recently penned a song called "My Own Soul's Warning" (from the album *Exploding the Mirage*, 2020) in which he asks,

> If you could see through the banner of the sun,
> Into eternity's eyes,
> Like a vision reaching down to you,
> Would you turn away?
> What if it knew you by your name?
> What kind of words would cut
> Through the clutter of the whirlwind of these days?

Let's take some deep breaths. Listen for God cutting through the whirlwind of these days. What is it that we might have forgotten, overlooked, or just plain missed? Don't turn away. Eternity is broadcasting.

> God, cut through the clutter so that I may fully hear that Eternity knows my name. Help me wire myself into your broadcast, becoming so connected that, at day's end, when I close my eyes, I may say the day was lived for *Your Glory Alone*. And that I missed nothing. Amen.

CHAPTER 8

ORIENTED X4

Back in grade school, my brother and I would ride our bicycles down our street to where the school bus would pick us up. We'd stash the bikes in the bushes behind a long wooden fence, and then after school we'd retrieve them and race each other home. During a particularly hotly contested race, a neighbor's dog bolted out in front of me. I avoided the dog, but in doing so I flew straight over my bike's handlebars. I was twelve. Bike helmets weren't yet a thing.

Unconscious, I was rushed in an ambulance to the hospital. I didn't wake up until the next day, and even that remains blurry. I have a vague disoriented recollection of adhesive stickers all over my arms, head, and shoulders with wires running to monitors. Once I awoke, I quickly deemed these medically unnecessary and pulled them all off. Nurses rushed in, trying to calm me as doctors followed and began to ask me questions that I ought to have known the answer to but didn't. Though awake and ornery, I still didn't know who I was, where I was, or how long I'd been out, and I certainly didn't know what had happened.

Tom Ehlers is a friend of mine. Tom's a paramedic. When Tom shows up to render care, he does what's called an A & O assessment to determine whether a person is "Alert and Oriented." A & O x3 means the person is alert and oriented to person, place, and time. They know who they are, where they are, and when it is. A & O x4 means the person can answer all that plus one more question—*do you know what's happened to you?*

In a time of pandemic in a deeply divided nation, we're disoriented—psychologically, spiritually, and perhaps even physically—as events swirl around us. We're left asking what's happened to us.

When I was very young, I'd go fishing with my grandfather. He was a skilled fisherman and exceptionally good at getting a hook out of a fish's mouth with his handy needle-nose pliers. Some of it was technique, and I sensed a lot of it was long experience, but what he stressed to me as he performed these operations was that you always need to have the right tools for the job you're trying to accomplish.

In this, our season of disorientation, the Psalms that God has dropped right in the middle of our Scriptures seem to me to be the right tool to reorient ourselves *x4*. The Psalms have an arresting way of saying what we're feeling. They have the power to stir us back toward who we are, cleansing us and leaving us more full-hearted as they do. They do this so effectively that it's worth asking how largely unknown lyrical poets writing some 3,000 years ago under largely unknown circumstances seem to be so acquainted with the sort of pain and disorientation we feel now in our modern world.

Bryan Doerries was in his twenties, pursuing an education focused on translating ancient Greek plays to English, when his girlfriend was diagnosed with cystic fibrosis. She fought valiantly but was soon placed in hospice, and, after a time, died at age twenty-four. Doerries had studied the plays of the Greek dramatist Sophocles before at length, but he said he simply didn't fully understand them until he'd suffered loss close up. After the death of his girlfriend, he read Sophocles with new eyes and ears.[1]

The play *Women of Trachis*, for instance, concerns the suffering and death of the hero Heracles and the plight of his son, Hylus, in caring for his father at the end of his life. When Doerries picked up Sophocles again in the context of great personal loss, he said it was if this ancient writer had penned a letter directly to him concerning what he'd gone through. Struck by this experience, he founded an organization, the Theater of War, a company of revolving actors that travels around the country presenting readings of Sophocles as well as biblical narratives like the book of Job to those who have lived through the modern equivalents of the sufferings and trials described in these historic texts. Doerries takes the story of the Trojan War, of Ajax and Achilles, to combat veterans, first responders, and health care workers who suffer from PTSD. He has presented *Women of Trachis* to audiences of hospice workers, terminal patients, and those in addiction clinics all over the country. The book of Job is played out before parents who have lost children and for audiences who have survived natural disasters. And in this, Doerries has found that time and time again, when people who know tragedy firsthand see their private struggles reflected in poetry, literature, and drama written thousands of years ago, something that triggers healing is unlocked inside them.[2]

That's precisely what the Psalms do as well. We see our own lives and predicament reflected there, and we feel less alone. We feel recognized, and hope flows from this recognition. *These stories tell us that God knows what life is like for us.* They tell us that what we're feeling now is not something that only we have felt but that, just as it's embedded in line after lyrical line, it's been felt by human beings for thousands of years. Just as the psalmist and the ancients ask, *How long, O God?* we ask it back and forth across the ages with them, holding the covenant promises of God and our present pain and disorientation upward to heaven with theirs. And somehow, together in this shared endeavor, we become more clear-eyed, more hopeful, and more alert to our present circumstances.

> God, help me to shed my disorientation, finding hope in common cause not only with my neighbors now but also with those who wrote and served and prayed for your help long ago. They were faithful. I too shall be. Amen.

CHAPTER 9

BEING WRONG, RIGHT

Max Tegmark is a physics professor at MIT who has written a book called *Our Mathematical Universe.*[1] In it, he explores the strange world of quantum mechanics and the true nature of reality. The book takes up ideas from the big—the possibility that our universe is just one of an infinite number of parallel universes in which each decision we make plays out in a series of alternate realities in what scientists call the multiverse—to the small—the notion that electrons and other subatomic particles can exist simultaneously in two or even many locations at the same time. The reason, Tegmark says, the world of quantum mechanics seems so bizarre and counterintuitive to us is that both the very, very big and the very, very small aren't domains to which our intuitions have been attuned by the evolutionary process. Natural selection rewarded with survival not our ancestors who pondered what was beyond the stars but our ancestors who contended well with the world at their own scale. That's all to say that, to understand quantum mechanics, we've got to be prepared to be wrong *a lot.* Tegmark goes so far as to say that if a developing quantum theory *isn't* counterintuitive to us, then we ought to be suspicious of it.

This is not only the case in quantum physics but in our faith as well. Just as we didn't evolve as humans to intuitively grasp the super-big and the super-small, God's ways are so different from ours that most of the time, our natural human instincts are reliably wrong when it comes to matters of faith. For instance, Christ's teachings about unconditional love are completely different from the *karma/cause and effect* world we're used to operating in most of the time. Likewise, the idea of forgiveness is so counterintuitive to our natural proclivity and survival instinct to strike back that if we're earnestly seeking to understand a God of lavish grace, we ought to be prepared to be wrong a good deal of the time.

This brings us to one of my favorite Bible characters, Jesus' mercurial disciple, Peter, whose main characteristics are that (1) he's devoted to Christ, and (2) he seems to be wrong a lot. And it might be the case that there's a correlation between these two characteristics. Recall the Gospel story in which Jesus has taken Peter, James, and John up onto a mountain to pray, and something extraordinary happens. The appearance of Jesus' face changes, his clothes become white like lightning, and then suddenly

Old Testament characters begin to appear; Moses and Elijah show up and speak with Jesus while the disciples, for some reason, fall completely asleep, only to suddenly awake as these heroes of the faith are departing. It's then that Peter proposes to Jesus that they make three little tents—one for Jesus, one for Moses, and one for Elijah. Then a cloud descends over them and a voice emerges, saying, "This is my son—my chosen one. Listen to *him*" (Matt 17:1-5).

One of the things I learned early in my law career was that if the judge is already leaning your way in a hearing, just keep quiet. If another lawyer elicits what you needed from a witness, there's no need to ask any more questions. Often in life, I think we take "saying nothing" off the table too quickly. There's a lot to be said for keeping silent sometimes, for quiet, for stillness. It's a lesson Peter should have thought about up there on the mountain. Instead, he's like a human gumball machine. Something momentous has happened and it's like somebody has dropped a quarter into the top of his head and the gumball descends. He feels like he has to weigh in. He means well, but he's so wrong-headed about it all that God has to show up via cumulus cloud to correct him, which leads us to this compelling question: *What kind of story is this, anyway?*

Is it a miracle? A vision? Is it a metaphor made super-vivid so we don't miss the point? I'm not sure, but I think the answer is *yes*.

I wear contact lenses most of the time. My vision is, as is the case for many of us, distorted. But if we think about it, our glasses, our contacts, are no more than another distortion. It's just that the original distortion, when combined with the second distortion, creates a *double* distortion that then produces a clearer picture. Mathematician Eric Weinstein makes the point that some of our clearest thinking—that is, our least distorted pictures of reality—arises when we use two lenses at once. First, we put on clear-eyed reason, a modern, rational lens full of rigor and "prove-it-to-me" thinking. Next, we put on a second lens—one that's open to wonder, to the transcendent, the miraculous, the mysterious. Even though the real truth must *be* one or the other, when we're willing to use both lenses simultaneously, or fluidly camping and decamping between the possibility of miracle and the likelihood of metaphor or vice versa, the two lenses combine to yield not incoherence but a more resonant sense of truth and as complete a picture of reality as we can find anywhere.

We can also embrace the Enlightenment and realize our Scripture is full of metaphor, art, allegory, poetry, theater, parable, and legend that reveal deep and honest truth. On the other hand, we shouldn't always rush to insist every miracle is a metaphor. We shouldn't be out to quell wonder and beauty or always be so quick to debunk the miraculous. We don't have to insist on demystifying everything. We can simply accept the tension of the two lenses, the double distortion, and explore in an ongoing dialectic between left brain and right both the rational and the transcendent, the historic and metaphorical, the art and the science. It's often at these intersections that we find God magnetized to truth, just waiting for us in an abiding stillness—which brings us back to Peter.

Peter's not a man of stillness. He's a man of action, and while we love this about the guy, this momentous event, whatever it was, should clearly have reduced him to silence. Instead he's suggesting an ill-conceived construction project. How, after three years of sermons and healings, adventures and conversations, can Peter not know the emergent truth about Jesus? How can Christ's closest confidant, his most earnest and devoted disciple, be wrong not just about this but about so much, so often?

What God seems to be demonstrating to us in Peter's life is that if we're truly devoted to Christ, we're likely to discover that we're not thinking nearly expansively or imaginatively enough about the power of grace, the import of love, and the realm of the invisible. Peter's life tells us that *if our religion tends to confirm what we think we're right about more than it teaches us what we're wrong about, we should be suspicious that we're not truly and actively seeking God as ardently as we might think we are.* If we're as dedicated to Jesus as Peter was, we should always be making counterintuitive discoveries of God through our deepening devotion to Christ.

Especially in a time of transition like the one we're in now, we ought to consider a switch in perspective from a notion of a Savior who bends and conforms to our preferred way of doing things to one who bends and conforms us to his. And Peter's life and this strange story in particular—whatever it is, miracle or metaphor—are telling us that perhaps the only way to learn it, as God told Peter there on the mountain, is simply to listen.

God, help me to ask and keep asking what my faith is telling me I'm wrong about rather than just looking to confirm what I'm right about. Amen.

CHAPTER 10

SCREAM

My son Charlie and I moved from room to room within the National Gallery of Art in Oslo, Norway, on one bright day a few summers ago. I'd thought the museum was lightly attended, but it only seemed that way because almost everyone had congregated in a single room around a single painting.

When he was five years old, Edvard Munch's mother died. When he was fifteen, his eldest sister died. When he was twenty-five, his father died. His other sisters went mad. Soon, Munch was living alone outside Oslo. And when he died in 1944 at the age of eighty, behind locked doors on the second floor of his home, a trove of his work was found: 1,008 paintings, 4,443 drawings, and more than 15,000 prints. Depressed yet madly prolific, Munch, ironically, is famous mainly for a single image. Some call it the Mona Lisa for our times. *The Scream*, though painted a century ago, captures how many of us see both our own age and this moment in particular. The painting is filled with deep anxiety and tense uncertainty amid an unsettling expanse of vibrating motion.

Many of us feel marooned in loneliness and mired in chronic stress. Others are gripped by addictions, depression, and despair, and there are a growing number of kids and teenagers suffering from these maladies. There's grief, worry, alienation—all occurring in the midst of this world's ever-humming, often distressing and disorienting velocity.

I should have known better than to pick up a book titled *Poems That Make Grown Men Cry*, but I did so not too long ago. Inside, I found a poem called "For Julia, in the Deep Water" by John N. Morris. In it, the poet describes his experience at his daughter's swimming lesson:

For Julia, In the Deep Water

The instructor we hire
because she does not love you
Leads you into the deep water,
The deep end
Where the water is darker—

Her open, encouraging arms
That never get nearer
Are merciless for your sake.

You will dream this water always
Where nothing draws nearer,
Wasting your valuable breath
You will scream for your mother—
Only your mother is drowning
Forever in the thin air
Down at the deep end.
She is doing nothing,
She never did anything harder.
And I am beside her.

I am beside her in this imagination.
We are waiting
Where the water is darker.
You are over your head,
Screaming, you are learning
Your way toward us,
You are learning how
In the helpless water
It is with our skill
We live in what kills us.[1]

Kindergarten's the deep end. Middle school's still deeper. Then high school. Pretty soon, it's just water all the way down, and we, as parents, our hearts straining taut, hope our children learn to swim by the time they can't touch bottom. But whether you're a kid or a grown-up or somewhere in between, what's clear is that, while people may go to Oslo to see *The Scream* because it's an iconic work of art, it's an iconic work of art because it tells us in a primal and elemental way what is lurking deep inside us.

The Gospel of Mark throws three miracle stories at us early on—Jesus calms a storm at sea, exorcises a demon, then raises a little girl back to life (Mark 4:35-41; 5:1-20; 5:21-43). Right in a row, we're told a single thing over and over again: *God resurrects*. Resurrects us from fear. Resurrects us in spirit. And resurrects us unto life. Hope issues from God constantly and continuously, bringing us back to life in every single way the world tries to kill us from the inside out.

After calming the seas, Christ says to his disciples, *"Why are you so timid?"* This storm story is clearly not just about the weather outside but about God's ability to tame our fear *inside*. Taking it like this puts in context what comes next: the story of the Gadarene demoniac. It sounds like a horror movie because it is one.

Let these images flicker through your mind: A battered boat carrying Jesus and a dozen shaken disciples is still a long way from shore when a series of shrieks pierce the darkness. Between the unsettling screams, over the lapping waves, the men then hear another disconcerting noise—a far-off chewing, snorting sound. In the moonlight on the cliffs above, they see a herd of filthy razorback boars rooting through the rocky soil along the ridge. As the boat crunches to a sudden stop, something emerges from the darkness. It's formidable, with strong and bloody hands. It's been among the tombs. Its face is gaunt and anguished; its body shredded; its mind gone.

Christ, standing his ground, demands its name. *"Legion,"* it howls back at him. The disciples, trembling, hear something about pigs as the demoniac sets off scrambling up the ravine, disappearing from view. An intense moment of silence follows. Then a faint rumble comes from above. Then louder. *Thunder.* They all look up as hundreds of hogs pour over the cliffs, following one after another, plunging into the sea in an endless series of dark thuds and heavy splashes. And when it all ends, the man—*a man anew*—comes down from the cliffs, resurrected in every way a person can be. What began as an absolute terror fest now screams hope back into the world. It screams that God's sympathy isn't inert, motionless, or theoretical but active, sure, and real.

Then comes the third story, and this time it's about a little girl. She has died. Her father and her mother weep beside her. But Jesus takes her hand and says to her, *Talitha Koum,* ("Little girl, to you I say, be arising"). The Scripture then gives us this: *Immediately the girl stood up and began to walk around (she was twelve years old).*

We all swim in the deep. Often, we stretch out our toes as far as they'll go, but we still can't touch bottom. It can induce fear. Life can be terrifying. Sometimes it even feels like God isn't here. But God *is here, especially now, when we're navigating through a storm.* Like a parent at a swim lesson, watching closely as we learn and even struggle, God is present—sometimes remaining still for a time, though I expect it's as hard for God to do nothing as it is for us when our child is scared. But whenever resurrection is truly needed in life, and even when it seems to end, God moves and finds us in the deep. God hears us when we scream and resurrects us in every way a person can be. So *be arising.*

> God, help me arise above all that makes me want to scream. Amen.

CHAPTER 11

DON'T BLINK

Lois Mae Blakey was born on March 11, 1924, and grew up in Tulsa, Oklahoma, as a small but spirited girl. In 1941, at age seventeen, on her first day of class at Oklahoma State, she met an athletic young man named Duane. A courtship began, and a few months later, when Duane joined the Army as the United States went to war, he asked Lois to marry him. Duane survived World War II, and when he returned, the young couple moved to Houston.

I didn't know Lois well, but after Duane's death I visited her at her home, a bright little apartment in a nice neighborhood where we sat down and spoke about her life and her memories. She recounted how she met Duane, her concern for him when he was serving his country overseas, and then how she and Duane raised their two remarkable boys, Paul who ran the 5000 meters in the 1976 Summer Olympics in Montreal, and Greg who worked with his dad and became a successful businessman. When she finished, Lois looked around her apartment at their pictures and her keepsakes, and then she leaned back and said something that struck me as humorous, deeply poignant, and undoubtedly true. "You know," Lois said, "you just blink and you're old."

Right now, time itself seems to be doing some weird things. Even when it seems like the days are trudging along, the weeks and the months might then accelerate. There's a sporadic nature to it all. When we look at important and anticipated life events approaching on the calendar, then watch them pass by in a way that leaves us empty—or not occur at all after being canceled—we feel a distinct sense of loss. In addition, in this time that sees us more restricted to home or limited in terms of activities, the days blur together and have a way of getting away from us. Life has a fleeting quality. But even now, we should acknowledge that it's the fleeting nature of life that instructs us most clearly that we're *always walking on holy ground.*

With this in mind, try a thought experiment: Imagine right now that you or you and your family are safe on the street, but your house is on fire. The fire is raging, but you have a chance, just a fleeting moment, to safely retrieve something crucial to you. *What would it be?* A scrapbook, a computer, your mother's china, your father's watch, your baseball glove?

Neuroscientist Sam Harris tells us that this is one way to look at reality. We're always continually waking up in the burning house of the present, deciding what to grasp, deciding what matters, what is worth paying attention to in each passing moment. Time is finite, and we can only give our true attention to one thing at a time. Harris points out that if we're not truly thinking of our attention as something valuable, we'll find ourselves pursuing and then holding on to something worthless most of the time. Our attention is our most important possession, the most valuable thing we have—in some sense the only thing we have. So don't blink. *Pay attention to your attention.* Give it to what matters.[1]

Rabbi Abraham Joshua Heschel, in his book called *Between God and Man*, writes that one of the most important words in all of Scripture is the Hebrew word *kadosh*, which translates as "holy" or "sacred."[2] He then points out that the first thing God declared *kadosh* in creation wasn't a thing like a mountain, a place like the garden, or a person like Adam or Eve. No. At the end of the creation story, "God blessed the seventh day, and made it holy." *Kadosh.* Holiness was first applied to time. Six days a week, Heschel writes, we live under the tyranny of things, but on the Sabbath we try to become attuned to holiness in *time.* The Sabbath is a gift from God that gives us the thing we need most—an awareness of time and its sacred nature, a time of rest, a moment to refocus, a day to reset, to reboot, to slow our lives down from their unsustainable velocities. To simply *be* rather than do. If you feel like you're missing something every time you blink, if life's going by too fast or seems too blurry, remember the Sabbath. God is there, inside this "palace in time," as Heschel calls it, just waiting for us.[3]

When we look at the question of whether we've borne this season well, or any season of challenge and difficulty in the future, a key point will be whether we used our time prudently and whether we refreshed and rebooted ourselves from time to time, as God not suggests but commands. I expect that simply being more aware of what we give our attention to day by day, being more conscientious about our spiritual health and God's design for us week by week, will give us a better sense of how life moves moment by moment and blink by blink.

> God, may I gather a better understanding for the rhythms of life by being more careful of what I give my attention to day by day; being more attuned to the most valuable uses of my time moment by moment;

and listening for your summons to observe the Sabbath blink by blink, consistent with the rhythms of my soul. Amen.

CHAPTER 12

TWO STORIES

My favorite children's book growing up was called *Fortunately*. The book had a simple plot that involved a boy named Ned who was invited to a surprise party, and it went like this:

> Fortunately, one day Ned was invited to a surprise party. Unfortunately, the party was in Florida and he was in New York. Fortunately, a friend loaned him an airplane. Unfortunately, the motor exploded. Fortunately, there was a parachute in the airplane. Unfortunately, there was a hole in the parachute.[1]

Admittedly a little dark for a child, the book goes on and on like this, back and forth between fortunate circumstances and unfortunate ones until Ned finally, fortunately, happily, gets to go to his party. But the book resonated with me because life seems just like this sometimes, as if there are two competing stories going on, constantly vying with one another for ascendancy in an almost binary fashion—*the fortunate and the unfortunate.*

The book of Acts, which concerns the early church, seems like this, especially as it nears its strange conclusion. Leaving Athens, fortunately, Paul was able to start churches in Corinth and Ephesus, and then he went to Troas. Unfortunately, while there in Troas, one night he went long preaching and a young man named Eutychus fell asleep, fell out of a window, and died. Fortunately, Paul restored him back to life. From Troas, Paul went next to Jerusalem, where, unfortunately, he was jailed. However, fortunately, this provided the opportunity for him to speak to several Roman leaders. Unfortunately, the Roman leaders ordered him to stand trial before Caesar. Fortunately, he got to leave jail by ship. Unfortunately, the ship wrecked. Fortunately, he survived and was washed ashore. Unfortunately, on shore he was bitten by a snake. Fortunately, it didn't affect him. Unfortunately, upon arriving in Rome, he was put under house arrest. Then, guess what? *The book of Acts just ends.*

> For two whole years Paul stayed there in his rented house and welcomed all who came to him and there he proclaimed the kingdom of God and taught the Lord Christ, with all boldness and unhindered! (Acts 28:31-32)

You may agree or disagree, but for such a momentous book, this curtain drop feels a little light as a climactic scene. And it certainly leaves us with loose ends. First, what happened to everybody? What happened to Paul? Second, I wonder about the use of the term "unhindered" as the last word. Paul is under house arrest in Rome. *Unhindered?*

When I run into a perplexity like this in the Bible, I remember the story of the wise rabbi and his new students. The rabbi was teaching the Torah, and they were launching into the book of Genesis—about Adam and Eve, Cain and Abel, Abraham and Isaac, Jacob and Joseph. The rabbi didn't get far before one of his students spoke up, asking, "Rabbi, did all this really happen?" To which the wise rabbi responded, *"It's what always happens."*

That is to say, perhaps Luke, the writer of Acts, is making a larger point. Maybe he's telling us that this story is much bigger than just what happens to Paul; that rather, this is God's story. Yes, Paul is in it, but it's God's story, and God's story can't be stopped or hindered. Ever. You can try, but what's about to happen as the book of Acts concludes is what *always happens* when people try to chain up the gospel truth.

A couple of years ago, my wife, Kelly, and I visited Ireland and toured a little town outside of Dublin called Kilmainham. It has a jail in which a number of Irish revolutionaries, including the leaders of the 1916 Easter Rising, were imprisoned and then executed by the orders of the British government. Next to the jail is a museum that tells the history, the story, of the prison. Walking through it, on the third floor I happened upon a room blocked by a couple of slender poles that didn't totally bar one's entrance. I peered in and saw several interesting photographs on the wall and even a video running on a screen. I thought to myself that if the museum's curators wanted to keep curious tourists out of what seemed like a compelling corner of their museum, they ought to apply a more robust effort than merely setting up a couple of skinny little poles. With this in mind, I went in and found myself in the middle of an exhibit about the life of the late South African leader Nelson Mandela.

It turned out the exhibit wasn't open to the public yet, but, before I was unceremoniously kicked out for breaking into the Mandela exhibit, the pictures I saw, the video I watched, and the power of the words I read reminded me that you can't imprison truth. It breaks out. Mandela was incarcerated in 1963 in South Africa, but during his twenty-seven years in prison, something else was happening, something spiritual, a sort of compounding accrual of moral capital in this imprisoned man that was then fully unleashed upon his release in 1990. He became unstoppable. Mandela was soon elected president of his country to effect and oversee the dismantling of the apartheid system that had jailed him, and then he even offered grace and forgiveness to his captors.

Luke's ending to Acts acknowledges that, yes, for all the world it may have looked as if Paul's chains hindered him from proclaiming the gospel— until you realize that we know Paul was wearing chains during this time under house arrest because he wrote a letter to his protégé, Timothy, that said so: ". . . this is my gospel, for which I am suffering even to the point of being chained like a criminal. But God's word is not chained" (2 Tim 2:8-9). And Paul didn't just write to Timothy. He wrote to everyone. To the Ephesians: "For it is by grace you have been saved through faith" (Eph 2:8). To the Colossians: "Christ in you, the hope of glory" (Col 1:27). To the Philippians: "I can do all things through Christ who strengthens me" (Phil 4:13). To the Galatians: "Let us not lose heart in doing good, for in due time we will reap if we do not grow weary" (Gal 6:9). And he wrote not just to them unhindered by distance *but also to us* across the ages, unhindered by *time*. What looked to human eyes like a hindrance or a limitation was God unleashing the gospel across both space *and* time.

What Luke is telling us is that when we nest our story inside of God's, our story, which, especially in seasons like this one, seems like one of fortune and misfortune vying back and forth for ascendancy instead becomes a part of God's larger story in which good *always* arises from bad, hope *always* emerges from despair, life *always* is reborn from death, and love eventually rolls over everything in its way. Because with God, *it's what always happens.*

God, may I nest my story inside of yours. Always.
Amen.

CHAPTER 13

DEMANDS OF THE SEASON

A few years ago, my son Hank was exploring possible choices for college. After touring the beautiful University of Chicago campus on a blustery but sunlit day, our family found itself at the corner of South Woodlawn Avenue and 58th Street in the Windy City. That's the address of the Robie House. The Robie House was designed and built around 1910 by Frank Lloyd Wright. It's the greatest existing example of a home designed in the Prairie School architectural style that Wright popularized. Horizontal lines, flat roofs, broad overhanging eaves—the Robie House is designated as a National Historic Landmark Site and was one of the first homes in the country placed on the National Register of Historic Homes. As an architectural buff in general and a fan of Frank Lloyd Wright in particular, I wanted to go inside. My two sons, specifically uninterested in Frank Lloyd Wright and quite reasonably indifferent to the arcane details of American architectural history, and also hungry, voted against my idea. My wife, Kelly, was marginally supportive as long as it didn't take too long.

There was a sign along the Woodlawn Avenue side of the house—I recall it said something about the tour entrance being on 58th Street, but I saw a door along the back at the end of the driveway of the house and headed that direction, as my plan was to just go inside and look around for a minute.

The Prairie School design and sensibility came about partly as a reaction against the assembly lines and mass manufacturing of the early twentieth century, so everything about the house was finely crafted, and the back door was no exception. It was beautiful, made of dark wood, walnut. Most of it, though, was glass, and it had a dark, polished metal handle. I turned it and pulled, but nothing happened. There was no click and I felt no engagement of a lock. The handle just turned and didn't open. Inside, I saw a little gathering near the door, so I kind of waved—happy to have stumbled upon some people with whom I could share my interest in Frank Lloyd Wright. However, none of them came over to help out. They all just looked back out the window with expressions of mild irritation. At that point, I tapped on the glass of this lovely door. Behind me, I heard, in sort of mortified voices, "Dad, we have to go around." Nonsense, I thought, and doubled down on my efforts, turning the handle again, waving, tapping. Now, a stern-looking older woman—protective and docent-like, cracked the door as one would if a suspicious person were on the back doorstep. What she said to me was, "Do you have tickets for the tour?" What she meant was, "You can't just walk through the back door of a Frank Lloyd Wright museum to haphazardly stroll around."

Behind me, my kids had fled. Kelly remained, presumably in case I needed to be bailed out of jail for breaking and entering a national historic landmark. In my defense, I just wanted to go inside for a few minutes. In their defense, they hold guided tours every half-hour.

It turns out that you can't just go in and look around in such an important place. *The place demands more of you.* They take it seriously because it's important inside, it's historic inside, and because of that, they ask that you to take it seriously too.

Just like some *places* demand more of us, some moments in *time,* some *seasons* in our lives, demand more of us as well. This season we've been trekking through seems to be one of those times. We'll undoubtedly look back on this moment as useful in the future with respect to measuring the levels of fortitude and grit we have inside of us. We're gaining a sense of knowledge concerning what we can endure in our families, our marriages, and ourselves. We're learning to handle pressure and where our emotional vulnerabilities might lie. We're getting to know what we're made of. And even if we didn't enter this season with a complete sense of its significance, now that we're inside, we should not be proceeding haphazardly or in a "business-as-usual" kind of way. Instead, we should be moving ahead thoughtfully, strategically, even rigorously, with a frame of mind that reflects not only the moment's significance but also the knowledge that how we're proceeding now is setting us on a certain trajectory for the future.

My friend J Hill is an artist, an art instructor, and the best person I know to lead you through a museum if you want to expand your knowl-edge and soul. His advice is to approach a museum with at least a little personal strategy in mind, that is, an idea of what you want to see and experience. He suggests picking maybe just three or four pieces to focus on rather than trying to consume everything at once. Trying to take in every-thing often leaves you walking away remembering little and being truly moved by nothing. I think this might be a good approach now too—to simplify our goals for this moment in time. To focus on just a few things that we want to be sure to accomplish in addition to the things that are required of us each day.

If we want to be able to say we've handled this season well—that we've done the best we can—then it's important to be aware of where we are, to have an idea of how we're moving through it, to not try to do too much at once, and to treat this challenging season like a momentous time, as the sacred place it is.

> God, help me think about where I am and to respect this place, to respect this time, and to use it with prudence, knowing that all of this and all that lies ahead is sacred ground. Amen.

CHAPTER 14

GOD IN LIVING COLOR

A furious squall came up, and the waves broke over
the boat, so that it was nearly swamped. Jesus was in
the stern, sleeping on a cushion. —Mark 4:37

I've seen the painting twice. The roiling otherworldly sea, electric aquamarine in color. A bright and shining glow of yellow above Christ's head. It mesmerized me both times. You may know the artist, the French Romantic Eugene Delacroix (1798–1863), whose painting, *Liberty Leading the People,* was repurposed by the popular British band Coldplay for the cover of their *Viva La Vida* album about a decade ago. In addition to famously painting Lady Liberty and the French tricolor on that canvas, Delacroix created an astonishing amount of religious art, more than one hundred pieces in all. He painted the scene from Mark 4, Christ asleep in a boat on a stormy sea, at least six times.

His *Christ on the Lake of Gennesaret,* also known as *Christ Asleep during the Tempest,* depicts a low-lying, lightning-lit vessel full of panicked apostles deep in high, blue-green seas. Two are rowing to save the boat, another is reaching for an oar lost in the waves, one has fainted, and most are simply shouting in desperation. Judas clutches desperately to a small money box at the bow, and Jesus sleeps peacefully on a cushion near the stern.

These days, it's not a huge leap to picture ourselves in the boat, isolated and vulnerable on stormy seas. However, the thing about the storms we're weathering now is that we don't have the option of physically shaking Jesus awake to calm the rough and tumbling waters around us. He's not physically with us to quiet the threatening skies above.

Thirty-three years after Delacroix created this painting, a young Dutch painter named Vincent van Gogh, quite taken with the work, sent a letter to his brother after viewing the painting at a Paris exhibition: "Oh, what a beautiful picture by Delacroix," van Gogh wrote of the reclining figure of Christ. "He, with his pale lemon halo, sleeping, luminous, within the dramatic violet, dark blue . . . on the terrifying emerald sea, rising, rising all the way up to the top of the frame." Van Gogh became fascinated by

Delacroix's use of color—how he could direct the eye, evoke emotion, and instill meaning with it. The son of a minister, van Gogh wrote that the halo around Christ spoke "a symbolic language through colour itself."[1]

Art historian Lauren Soth, citing van Gogh's letters and his avowed admiration for Delacroix (and in particular this painting), believes he took up this symbolic language when he painted *Starry Night over the Rhone* in 1888.[2] You're likely familiar with it. The work depicts a couple walking hand in hand on the bank of the river under a brilliant, star-decked night sky. Van Gogh, using Delacroix's dramatic Prussian blue and citron yellow, then paints the bursting evening stars above, echoing Delacroix's Christ-crown halo, symbolizing the presence of the Divine.

Van Gogh, who once served as a missionary pastor, painted biblical scenes himself and wrote of religious and spiritual matters in his letters and notebooks almost as much as he wrote about his art. In *Starry Night over the Rhone*, he seems to be saying that our yearning for consolation from God can be fulfilled, just as Christ was present for his bewildered disciples, if we will simply *awaken* to God's presence. As heaven commingles with earth in his painting, God is with us within the vast array of elusive invisibilities all around us. In beauty. In the night sky. In vibrant heavenly light. In art. In love and in the consolation of friends. *Awaken*, Vincent is saying, to God in living color.

> God, when I examine the evidence, between the two of us it's me who is asleep in the storm, not you. Help me to wake up a little bit more so that I can see what I suspect: that you are closer than I think, more powerful than I believe, and more intimate than I can imagine. Help me to apprehend more fully what I deduce from the themes of the gospel and the beauty of sublime art—that heaven commingles with earth, that your love is as fierce as the stars, that the squalls will diminish, and that trundling waves shall not swamp the boat. Widen my eyes to the consolation on offer to me today, in living color. Amen.

CHAPTER 15

"EVENTS, DEAR BOY, EVENTS."

When asked about the greatest challenge a leader faces, British Prime Minister Harold MacMillan, who served the crown during the Cold War, is said to have answered, *"Events, dear boy, events."* Normal life seems a long way off, and we continue across unexplored territory each day. In a sense, this is always the case. There's always something. "Events, dear boy, events."

But here's the thing: God can see ahead where we can't. In each moment when we feel fear and doubt about what might be over the horizon, God encourages, instructs, and even demands each of us to express our anxiety, our uncertainty, our disappointment, our grief, and even our anger with pure and ruthless honesty through our prayers. This honesty, this exercise—when conducted thoughtfully—is something that not only spiritually but also psychologically prepares us for what's ahead.

Try praying out ahead of your day, not to try to exert personal control over everything, as that's not possible, but to rehearse your trust before God. In the morning, look ahead over what you're likely to face and become self-aware of the potential obstacles. Think about and pray for those you will encounter. Consider, in God's presence, your responses and your expectations for yourself. Make a game plan for your day with God in prayer. Of course, it's not likely to play out as you think ("Events, dear boy, events"), but there will be a sense in each moment that you and God have been there before. You'll be more prepared in a practical sense, and you'll feel God's presence within you more palpably. While none of this is any sort of guarantee against surprise or defeat, it is quite literally learning how to trust in God's vision more than simply your own.

It seems like maybe this is what Jesus did. Even on the cross, we remember that Jesus himself prayed aloud the opening line of what we know as Psalm 22 when he cried out, "My God, My God, why have you forsaken me?" For a long time, I thought this was the moment that Jesus broke, felt abandoned by God, and was expressing, confessing even, that he'd somehow lost God's eyes, God's vision, in this moment. But if you read the whole psalm, this doesn't seem to be the case. It was not unusual at the time for a rabbi to speak the first lines of Scripture, in effect invoking the entirety of the passage. It appears that this is what Jesus was doing. The excerpts from Psalm 22 below give insight as to what Jesus was thinking, praying, and seeing played out before him while on the cross. It reads like a script of the scene and sets out what must have been in his head as he was suffering, enduring, fighting through the day. When it was most bleak and seemed to his followers that the plan to save the world had completely collapsed, God saw out in front, ahead of the current moment, and Jesus relied on that as he prayed this psalm. Attend the remarkable arc of the narrative as you read.

> My God, my God, why have you forsaken me?
> Why are you so far from saving me,
> so far from my cries of anguish?
> My God, I cry out by day, but you do not answer,
> by night, but I find no rest. . . .
>
> All who see me mock me;
> they hurl insults, shaking their heads.
> "He trusts in the LORD," they say,
> "let the LORD rescue him." . . .
>
> I am poured out like water,
> and all my bones are out of joint.
> My heart has turned to wax;
> it has melted within me. . . .
>
> Dogs surround me,
> a pack of villains encircles me;
> they pierce my hands and my feet.
> All my bones are on display;
> people stare and gloat over me.
> They divide my clothes among them
> and cast lots for my garment.
> But you, LORD, do not be far from me.
> You are my strength; come quickly to help me. . . .
>
> For he has not despised or scorned
> the suffering of the afflicted one;
> he has not hidden his face from him
> but has listened to his cry for help.
> From you comes the theme of my praise in the great assembly;

before those who fear you
I will fulfill my vows. . . .

All the ends of the earth
will remember and turn to the LORD,
and all the families of the nations
will bow down before him,
for dominion belongs to the LORD
and he rules over the nations. . . .

Posterity will serve him;
future generations will be told about the LORD.
They will proclaim his righteousness,
declaring to a people yet unborn:
He has done it!

Just as God was surely with Jesus as he prayed in the worst circumstances imaginable, God is with us as we pray every day. We must rely on that. Even when things look like a train wreck ahead of us, God sees out in front and is with us. So let us offer this prayer of trust before a loving and graceful God as the arc bends and as matters play out, in the midst of the events we're suffering, enduring, and fighting through now, as well as in all the events ahead.

> God, it's the events that get to me. I can't see ahead. As Christ prayed from the cross in what seemed like desperate, forlorn doubt, his words were instead clear evidence of an arc of trust and reliance. I can't see ahead right now. Threats hover over me. Formidable risk encircles me, and its mouth is wide against me. I am uncertain of my future. God, I confess that I fear and am unsure of what's next myself. Help me to pray ahead, to read ahead. I trust that you see all. As Jesus relied on you, I trust you also. Be with me as events unfold. Fold me in your care. Amen.

CHAPTER 16

TRIALS

My uncle, Larry Funderburk, is an attorney and was my law partner for a long time. One of his main clients was the Werner Ladder Company. For many years, whenever Werner was brought into a lawsuit, they'd call Larry to defend them. One of these cases involved a ten-foot aluminum stepladder and a man named Boyd who claimed he was on the ladder when one of its side rails bent, causing him to fall and sustain an injury. Werner, on the other hand, contended that the ladder was strong and that Mr. Boyd must have lost his balance, causing the ladder to tip over, and that the side rail bent only when he fell on top of it.

Werner sent a young engineer down from headquarters to help Larry try the case and was keen on the idea of Larry, in a dramatic courtroom presentation during trial, demonstrating to the jury the strength of the ladder. He proposed getting a ladder identical to the one in question, and—in the presence of the jury—sawing deeply into two of the ladder's braces that were designed to give it strength and stability, then proceeding to saw the side rail in question halfway through as well. With that done, the young engineer then proposed having four people climb up onto the ladder to show that it wouldn't collapse even in this drastically compromised condition.

Larry said, "No way. We're not doing that. It's too risky." But the engineer wouldn't take no for an answer, so finally, against his better judgment, Larry relented, got the judge's permission for the demonstration, and the next day he moved the equipment into the courtroom. You can imagine how the jury began leaning forward in their seats as the representatives of the defense sawed the braces through and then the side rail. The chamber grew quiet when the engineer asked Larry's co-counsel, a man who weighed 250 pounds, to climb up onto the ladder. Then the engineer himself climbed up, and then he asked the court reporter up, and finally, with three people already on the steps of ladder, he motioned to Larry to come on over. Larry, mind you, was never in favor of any of this in the first place, but, hiding his nervousness, he rose from counsel's table and stepped onto the ladder with his heart pounding. If the ladder collapsed, they would not only lose the case but his legal career—marked until now by professionalism, considerable dignity, and admirable restraint—would be remembered only for one of the most embarrassing courtroom blunders in the history of Texas jurisprudence. As the seconds wore on, I was told that you could have heard a pin drop in the courtroom. They remained there for several minutes, but the ladder held. They finished the case and the verdict came back in their favor.

Trials bring things to a climax, to a place of clarity, to a moment of truth that, often in stark relief, reveals the essence, the true character, of a particular controversy, event, or, in some cases, a person. That's what they're meant to do.

There's a moment in Scripture that's like that. It's a trial, but a strange one. It was held at night and broke all the rules that were supposed to be followed in such a proceeding. Jesus had been arrested, and witness after witness called to testify against him had cratered. His opponents' accusations were crumbling, and yet Jesus remained in danger, on trial for his life. The high priest, Caiaphas, stepped forward and, face to face with his Galilean nemesis, asked him a question: *"Are you the Messiah?"*

Now that's a moment of truth. If trials are meant to bring things to a climax, a place of clarity, a moment of truth, then it's arrived. The jury is sitting at the edge of their seats, and surely you could have heard a pin drop if there were such a thing.

Let's engage in our thought experiment again. Let's project ourselves forward in time, even as we remain in the present, and ask, *how do we want to look back on this time of trial?* Will we be able to say we did as well as we could? Did we persevere with both faith and courage? Did we use our time prudently? Did we develop additional personal grit and grace while forbearing one another's faults during this season? Did we weave social fabric or were we a part of its unraveling? We desperately want to answer these questions in the affirmative, but in the midst of our trials it's hard.

So, when your heart is pounding and you're not sure if your ladder will hold; if in the midst of this trial you're not sure your spirit will hold; if you're exhausted, broken, and at the end of your rope, then remember Jesus' answer to the chief priest's question at his own moment of truth. When you don't feel nearly strong enough against the day; when you're lost, fed up, or confounded; when you're at the brink and looking down into the abyss, certain that you're just not up to face your own moment of truth, remember the words Jesus spoke in his: "I am."

God, give me strength and courage to contend with
the world, to battle exhaustion, and to endure the trials

ahead. I will listen for your voice such that when I ask if you are with me in my moment of truth, I hear the words Jesus spoke at his: *I am.* Amen.

CHAPTER 17

THE NIRVANA FALLACY

"What have you learned during this time of strain and struggle?"

I was recently asked this question, so I started in on my list. First, I'm now a Zoom wizard. I've got a little makeshift studio, and I procured from Target some decent lighting so that on screen, I don't look totally cave-bound. Second, I hear "Greg, you're on mute" a lot less now. So I've almost got that down. Third, I keep learning new stuff. I heard recently that if you keep a peppermint in your mouth when you're wearing glasses and a mask, there's no fog and, as a bonus, your breath stays minty fresh.

But there's a difference between "What I've Learned during the Pandemic" and "What I've Taken to Heart during the Pandemic." What I've taken to heart starts with something called the Nirvana Fallacy. The Nirvana Fallacy is not an argument against the ancient Buddhist belief in an enlightened state, nor does it posit the superiority of Pearl Jam as the best Seattle grunge band of the 1990s. No. The Nirvana Fallacy refers to our human tendency to assume that there's a perfect solution for every problem. It suggests that, when faced with a problem, if we just make the right binary choice, do this or do that, then good things will follow. Our problems will be solved. Nirvana can be reached. What I've always suspected, and what I now know, is that life is far more complicated than that, and, more often than not, there *is* no perfect path or perfect answer to many problems. This seems especially to be the case these days. *Right now, it feels more like we're navigating the open seas than like we're on a well-paved road, looking for the right turnoff.* Sometimes life is about choosing among bad options and then keeping on.

As I take this to heart, several things follow. First, we need to be extra graceful to one another right now. This is countercultural, so it should feel right to ardent Christ-followers, but it's still hard. Sometimes choosing between or among the bad options is a close call, and we should be robust instead of stingy in our offering of grace to others in these situations.

Coaching little league baseball spun off a lot of lessons for me over time, mostly about patience, the importance of community, and a better perspective on competition. (You'll notice that I didn't say I *learned* all the lessons, but they were definitely offered to me throughout more than a decade of memorable seasons.) During this time, I also came to understand something important about decision-making and living philosophically with your decisions. Consider this situation that arises commonly on the baseball diamond: the pitcher on the mound is struggling, and the manager has a decision to make—leave the pitcher in or remove him from the game. Let's play this out. You leave him *in*. When the next batter gets a hit, it's generally held that the manager must have made the wrong decision. And I suppose that's fair. But what's often *not* taken into account is the possibility that the relief pitcher may have given up the hit as well. This error in analyzing alternative histories isn't limited to baseball. Our eager criticisms of decision-makers often employ such incomplete and inexact logic. It's usually unfair and exemplifies a stingy brand of grace. Let's do better.

Second, we ought to be extra patient with each other. We're all trying to make the best possible decisions for our families and our communities with the temperaments we have, the resources at our disposal, and the navigational information at hand. When we're not on a road with a series of forks but instead on the open seas, the best strategy is to keep breathing deeply and to keep tacking toward shore, but even as we're doing this, we've got to be prepared to make an ongoing series of fluid course-corrections. Sometimes, taking up a flexible posture and a patient attitude like this is a sort of wisdom in and of itself.

Steven Browning Sample served as the president of the University of Southern California from 1991 to 2010. Sample, who died in 2016, may be best known as the author of a book titled *The Contrarian's Guide to Leadership*.[1] (He and his wife, Kathryn, donated all the book's royalties to a scholarship fund for USC undergraduates. *Fight on!*) Sample's counterintuitive lessons include intriguing gems like these never make a decision today that can reasonably be put off until tomorrow; think gray—don't form opinions if you don't have to; the best leaders don't keep up with the popular media and the trades; know what hill you are willing to die on (and keep its exact location to yourself); and, finally, you can't copy your way to the top. These and other pieces of advice in the book all seem to speak in favor of patience, restraint, independence, and a sophisticated and supple way of thinking that recognizes the Nirvana Fallacy. Further, they present to us lessons to take to heart especially when sailing on open seas.

God, in a season of rough and open seas, help me to take the right lessons to heart, doubling down on grace for others. Give me patience in trying circumstances, as I keep my eyes open to the best way forward, ready to make a series of course-corrections under your good guidance. Amen.

CHAPTER 18

SMALL POTATOES AND ZINNIAS

Ken Chafin was the pastor of South Main Baptist Church in Houston for twelve years. After leaving, he led a church in Louisville, Kentucky. In his retirement, Ken returned to South Main, taught a Sunday school class, and wrote poetry. Sadly, he died of leukemia only a few years after coming back. One of his poems, "A Rhythm for My Life," can be read on a plaque outside Westmoreland Chapel on South Main's campus. Tucked into the middle of the poem you'll find these lines:

> Let there be a celebration of life,
> the building of relationships,
> and the nurturing of others.
> Let there be unhurried strolls in the woods,
> quiet mornings spent on the pond,
> poking around country roads.
> Afternoon naps in the porch swing,
> leisurely meals with friends,
> chickadees fed and zinnias grown.

When Kelly and I joined South Main, Dr. Chafin had just returned to our church. As a new couple, we were without a "small platoon"—without a community where we could weave and become caught up in the sort of crucial social fabric a newly married couple needs as they set out to start a family. Dr. Chafin was a hero of mine—a champion of moderate Baptist thought, independent of mind, and a legendary preacher—so when he asked us if we wanted to join his new class, it was an easy "yes." The next Sunday, we attended for the first time. Kelly and I were both drawn in by his salty style and dialogue-driven teaching, but what was going through my mind was this: that with his experience and wisdom, he ought to be speaking to large audiences full of important leaders and influencers. *Why was this brilliant guy wasting his legendary teaching skills and talents on a little group of five, six, or seven couples?*

I mean, what could one person accomplish over a period of just a few short years of dedicating his time, focus, energy, and attention to a dozen or so young men and women who didn't even know what they were doing in life yet? We were small potatoes.

But that's how it went. Week after week, we sat in class and received his wisdom, delivered with a raw honesty and a platitude-free sense of authenticity and clarity. He built relationships among us, nurturing us along. He invited us to his farm outside of Brenham to stroll along and poke around country roads, spend afternoons on the porch talking, and share leisurely meals with friends. There were flowers on the table, zinnias perhaps. There might even have been some chickadees. Or maybe *we* were the chickadees.

The late pastor and writer Eugene Peterson, in a speech given as a part of the Kistemaker Academic Lecture Series, tells us that God's character was revealed to us when Christ dwelt not over us, not around us, but among us.[1] Peterson pointed out that in Jesus' short but instructive life, he committed himself not to an easy, general, or idealized fondness or beneficent rule over a large population of people but to the close companionship of a small band of not terribly impressive men and women. That is, Jesus— and these are Peterson's words—committed himself to "small potatoes," going for "the jugulars of the real and specific persons God put into his influence . . . committing himself to the companionship of real people and the transformation of all the motives and modes of these few souls." And he did it with only time, truth, and love.[2]

The lives of Ken Chafin and Eugene Peterson point out to us what I suspect Jesus was like—undoubtedly good in a crisis but fully immersed in the everyday texture of real people's lives. So it follows that if we want our lives to reflect and advance the gospel, its evidence must emerge in the midst of our everyday lives, as Peterson wrote, in "getting kids off to school, deciding what to have for dinner, dealing with the daily droning complaints of work associates, watching the nightly news on TV, making small talk at coffee break."[3]

As we move through a hard season, without many of the normal rhythms of coming and going each week, including coming and going to church, it's getting more and more clear to me that our lives are not made up of a long series of worldly weekday moments interrupted every seventh day by a spiritual Sunday. No. The sacred is perhaps most reliably embedded and on offer to us in our "small potato" moments.

> God, help me to be a person who gently but readily
> enters into the everyday sounds and silences of each
> Monday; poised to receive the holy offerings inside

of Tuesday; a person who looks for and finds you woven mysteriously in and through the loose fabric of Wednesday; committing myself to the small potato moments of Thursday; ready to listen and sit patiently with every eternity-bound human I encounter on Friday; and excited to look for the zinnias on Saturday. Amen.

CHAPTER 19

PLAN IT OVER

My son Hank attends college at USC in Los Angeles. We met up in Seattle a couple of years ago aiming to visit Mt. Rainier. We rented a car, got some sleep in the hotel, and the next morning I typed "Mt. Rainier National Park" into my phone's navigation app, chose a route, and we headed out of town. But about sixty miles into our ninety-minute drive, we found ourselves on a narrow, icy, almost deserted road. I began to suspect that where we thought we were going and where the navigation system thought we were going were two different places. When Hank checked, he pointed out that I'd routed us to the Carbon River entrance of the park instead of the more popular, picturesque one located at a place called Nisqually Falls. I replied that I was sure there'd be some great sites along the Carbon River route and suggested we just keep going.

The record, if reviewed closely, will reflect that neither Hank nor any of the travel guides agreed with my plan. Nevertheless, we soon found ourselves in front of Ranger Stephanie, a friendly park ranger assigned to the Carbon River entrance of the park. Though affable and knowledgeable about the place, she was not an ardent enthusiast for its attractions and encouraged us to turn around. "Nisqually Falls," she said, "shouldn't be missed." Although Hank was standing directly behind me, I could feel him shaking his head as I thanked Ranger Stephanie for her helpful insight.

What do we do when where we thought we were going and where our lives have taken us turn out to be two different places? What do we do when, because of a bad decision, a detour brought on by illness or accident, or just the general misfortune a pandemic brings, our lives spin off in an unwanted direction? What would God have us do when our lives take a sharp turn off the expected path?

The main thing that most of us remember about the Old Testament "riches to rags to redemption" story of Joseph is that he had a Technicolor dream coat of some sort. This coat of many colors, a gift from his doting father, was the start of Joseph's detours. He was thrown into a hole by his jealous brothers and then sold to slave traders. He next rose to prominence in the house of Potiphar before his life took another sharp downward turn into prison when he was wrongly accused of sexual assault. In jail, though, he rose again to become head trustee, administrating the whole prison. He found a way out as a dream interpreter and eventually ended up second in command to Pharaoh as a famine arose in the land. Against all odds, Joseph saved the very brothers who had set out to kill him almost two decades before, as well as their starving families and, in effect, all of God's chosen people (along with the Egyptians). The story is a compelling fourteen-chapter novella thematically focused on how to navigate the detours of our lives.

The night before our trip to see Ranger Stephanie and Mt. Rainier, Hank and I checked into the hotel in Seattle. I was sorely disappointed. When I'd made the room reservation online, the pictures suggested the room had a beautiful view of nearby Puget Sound. Although once we were in the room we could see a slice of the water way off in the distance, the predominant features through the window were a giant run-down building and a construction zone. If the photographer who took the website picture had adjusted the camera just a little, we would have seen the true and not-so-attractive reality of our room's view. Most of us have had an experience like that.

This works the other way around too. We can be in an ugly or difficult place in our lives, but if we're able to pull back just a little and see a wider, fuller picture, we will see that the story we think we're in isn't all there is. Often when it seems like we're in a pit in the middle of the desert as Joseph was, it's important to remember that there are always two stories going on—one we see and one we don't see. When we're in a detour, we see with our limited human vision, and things may truly look bad, even bleak, even hopeless. But our faith tells us that even if we can't quite see it, there's always a second story going on. That second story may remain invisible to the human eye for weeks, for months, for years, sometimes even for decades, as it was in Joseph's case, but there's always a second story going on—one through which God is working out God's own redemptive purposes both in our world and in our lives. My explanation of this phenomenon is that God is, you know, God.

Do you remember those overhead projectors teachers used in middle school? They would write something on a transparency sheet and then project it on a screen at the front of the class and do an equation or diagram a sentence. Get that picture in your mind—a clear sheet on which your life's plan is drawn out. Whether we mess up our own picture, or someone else does, or a pandemic does, or something else unforeseen does, it's God's nature—God's rescuing, redeeming business—to lay another transparency, a second page on top of ours until, together with ours, a new story emerges. As we work in conjunction with God's purposes, new lines appear, rerouting the plot. Loose ends are tied off in unexpected ways, and paths are linked back up into some new, beautiful, unexpected, and redemptive story. *Trust in this. Trust in the second story.*

God, just as Joseph said to his brothers at the end of his story, "You planned harm against me, but God planned it over for good," let me speak the same words into the misfortune of the pandemic and any other nemesis to be faced ahead: I will trust in the second story, your redemptive one that always plans over mine for good. Amen.

CHAPTER 20

GET OUT OF YOUR OWN WAY

Song Exploder is podcast created by a man named Hrishikesh Hirway. Here's how it works: Hrish interviews a musical artist, one each week, about a particular song they've written. The writer talks about their craft, the derivation of the song, and a little about its meaning. You get to listen in as the song is being born. You get to see the song come together. I'm not sure why Hrish called his podcast *Song Exploder*, but it makes me think of an Ikea diagram for building a shelf or futon. The instruction sheet includes what's known as an "exploded drawing" that helps you see how the thing is built, how it all fits together.

In one of the episodes, Jeff Tweedy, the lead singer and lyricist for the band Wilco, describes a process by which he composes. Tweedy says often another member of the band develops a sonic idea—a riff on the guitar or a song fragment on the piano—and Tweedy listens along as his bandmate plays it. He hums or sings nonsense words through the notes until he finds a melodic line. There are still no words at this point, but he follows the melody he's located and just places his voice where he thinks it fits within the riff or fragment. Tweedy then records what he calls a "mumble" track. The idea is not to think too hard at that stage. He might glance at one of his notebooks, where he keeps his random thoughts and observations, and then begin to experiment, moving things around, getting a little closer to something real that's inside him.

"I just keep going," Tweedy says, "trusting something will come out if my ego isn't trying to direct all the meaning." He adds,

> Your ego really isn't that interested in what's inside of you. Your ego's interested in presenting an idealized version of yourself out in the world. And what's really inside you, *trying* to get out, only cracks through when you get out of the way. I trust that a lot more than I trust myself. I trust the process to get to something honest, vulnerable, authentic and real. When it's hard and not making a lot of sense, you just have to get out of the way.[1]

Often in difficult spots in life when things are hard and not making a lot of sense, we find it difficult to get out of our own way. We want to *do* something, *fix* something, *force* a change, *turn* the page. We are so reluctant to just sit and rest and *think about* what we're *thinking about*. Most of us have a distinct bias toward movement.

Zat Rana is a writer who describes his work as "playing at the intersection of philosophy, science, and art. Trying to be less wrong."[2] In an article about mathematician, philosopher, and theologian Blaise Pascal (who did everything he did in all these fields before dying at age thirty-nine), Rana writes,

> Right before his death, he was hashing out fragments of private thoughts that would later be released as a collection by the name of *Pensées*. While the book is mostly a mathematician's case for choosing a life of faith and belief, the more curious thing about it is its clear and lucid rumination on what it means to be human. It's a blueprint of our psychology long before psychology was deemed a formal discipline. . . . One of its most famous thoughts aptly sums up the core of his argument: "All of humanity's problems stem from man's inability to sit quietly in a room alone."[3]

Rana observes that we never learn the art of solitude. "We now live," he writes, "in a world where we're connected to everything except ourselves." Rana's solution, taking a page from Pascal, is to let solitude—and even boredom—take us where it wants. He calls this the most important life skill that no one teaches us.

Pascal's diagnosis, Rana's unspooling of the idea, and Tweedy's advice about trusting the process and getting out of our own way are all related to consciousness and possibly even prayer. I'm becoming more and more convinced that God, in addition to being Love, Creator, and, well, God, is also *Consciousness*—that is, God resides in our consciousness, or, better put, we reside in God's, but ours is so busy, cluttered, messy, overactive, and scared that we rarely pause and endeavor to rest our consciousness in God's. Though this rest is on offer to us all the time, we don't prioritize it or bring ourselves to do it.

Maybe if we pictured the exploded diagram and better comprehended that our little lives and our little consciousnesses reside securely within God's, we would realize that what's inside us—what's honest, vulnerable, authentic, and real; what's trying to get out into the world—only cracks through when we get out of our own way and rest all that we have and all that we are inside of God.

> God, may I make room for solitude, even boredom. May I set aside time to sit quietly in a room alone, to locate my little consciousness securely inside yours, and then to let go, get myself out of the way, and let you crack through. Amen.

SELF-CARE

"Radical self-care is quantum." —Anne Lamott (from "12 Truths I Learned from Life and Writing," TED2017)

CHAPTER 21

NUMBER 8, TODAY

One of my favorite movies is *Apollo 13*. Maybe you're familiar with the film if not the actual events of the mission. Commanded by astronaut Jim Lovell, *Apollo 13* was forced to abort its planned moon landing after a routine stir of an oxygen tank ignited damaged wire insulation inside the service module, causing an explosion. The crew was forced to loop around the Moon without landing, and then—through remarkable engineering work on the ground and steady nerves in space—return safely to Earth.

The movie does a terrific job of moving between the harrowing experiences of Lovell and his crew and the tenacity shown by members of mission control. Many of us in Houston, Texas, where I live, have grown tired of the film's signature line—say it with me: "Houston, we have a problem." But it's pretty iconic. Even so, that's not the line in the film's script that keeps popping into my head over and over these last few months, in this strange season of adversity. It's two other lines.

After the explosion, a flurry of activity ensues both in the spacecraft and at mission control, until Flight Director Gene Kranz, played by Ed Harris, focuses everyone's attention and efforts with these words: "Quiet down. Stay cool . . . alert your support teams. Wake up anyone you need. . . . Work the problem, people."[1]

The next line that has stayed with me and keeps entering my mind these last few months is given voice deeper into the story as the astronauts are still a long way from home. They are dealing with a multitude of oxygen, navigation, and power problems. Astronaut Jack Swigert, played by Kevin Bacon, begins to fear that the reported telemetry they've been given by NASA for reentry is off and that, if followed, it will lead their craft to either skip off of the earth's atmosphere or to burn up in a fiery disaster upon reentry. While this problem is obviously crucial, Lovell, played by Tom Hanks, responds to Swigert with some irritation: "Alright, there are a thousand things that have to happen in order. We're on number—8. You're talking about number 692."

As we face each day, it's easy, even natural, to get overwhelmed and anxious with all the problems and uncertainties we're facing. They're legion, most of them unprecedented, but what tends to tame my own agitation in the ongoing forging ahead into the unknown is to break things down into bits, not too big and not too small, and then consider what's before me each day. There's an art to it, and we need to get the hang of it as we further integrate this pandemic and its aftermath into our lives.

. . . there are a thousand things that have to happen in order. We're on number—8. You're talking about number 692.

If I can't hear the calm, cool, and collected voice of Commander Jim Lovell telling me this, I can at least hear actor Tom Hanks. Focus on number 8 today, or maybe 8 through 12. When 8 through 12 are done, maybe take on a few more; maybe you'll get to 20 today. It doesn't make. sense to take up number 8 and then number 692, or even worse, number 8 through 692 all at once.

Yes, many, many things are ahead, and a lot of them are important; some of them are crucial. But there's a sequence, and they can't all be done at once. They can't all be done today. Trying to do so just leads to a panicky feeling that you'll never get home.

Quiet down. Stay cool . . . alert your support teams. Wake up anyone you need. . . . Work the problem, people.

Just work the problem that's in front of you today. And get some backup. Alert your support teams. Wake up anyone you need. This sequenced, step-by-step, bit-by-bit approach, supported ably on the ground, got the *Apollo 13* astronauts home from the dark coldness of distant space. I bet it works here on Earth too.

> God, sometimes I feel as though a dozen problems are coming at me like giant meteors. I know from experience that all but one or two will veer off and away before they reach me, and the others I can typically deal with as they get closer. Yet I worry about all of them. May I hear your voice echo inside of these words: *"There are a thousand things that have to happen in order. We're on number 8. You're talking about number 692."* Help me to quiet down, stay cool, alert my support team, and wake up anyone I need. And be with me as I work the problem. Amen.

CHAPTER 22

EQUANIMITY

The mind is its own place and in itself, can make
a Heaven of Hell, a Hell of Heaven. —John Milton,
Paradise Lost, Book I

For there is nothing either good or bad, but thinking
makes it so. —William Shakespeare, *Hamlet*, Act 2,
sc. 2

Shut up, brain, or I'll stab you with a Q-tip! —Homer
Simpson

I suspect that Shakespeare and Milton are right. How we think about and consider our experience within our minds makes all the difference. We hear that we should ground ourselves in gratitude. We should meditate, be still, reframe events in our lives to see the bigger picture, find balance, peace, and calm, all the while funneling our energy into the good and noble. *I know this.*

But unfortunately, more often *I'm like Homer.* My mind ponders things on its own whether I like it or not, and my feelings are even worse. I feel what I feel until I don't feel it anymore. I can't stop it. I get caught in a loop. I get stuck.

Jesus tells us, "Don't worry about tomorrow. Tomorrow will worry about itself. Each day has enough trouble of its own" (Matt 6:34). He is wisely encouraging us to live each day in the present, trusting that God loves us. But as much as I try, I'm not wired to be a "now" person, and further, the way he puts it, tomorrow doesn't sound like it's going to be a picnic either. And with all that's been going on—a pandemic, confinement, and no solid timeline to grasp, how can I be expected to stop my mind from running and worrying? *Just give me the Q-tip.*

Dr. Molly Colvin is an assistant professor of psychology at Harvard Medical School. In a recent online article, she writes about the "fight or flight" mode our brains enter under acute stress. From an evolutionary standpoint, this works superbly to help us avoid predators, but when the stress we face is more chronic in nature as it has been lately, things become more problematic. Chronic stress, she says, leads our brains into a fog, but she hastens to add that while frustrating, this *brain fog* may be a good thing. It's a signal that what we're experiencing is abnormal. It prevents us from taking on too much or from trying to move too fast in uncertain times. "The fog," Colvin writes, "forces our hands and minds to be still so that fear, grief, and sadness may visit."[1]

I once heard a preacher say that if we find ourselves in a time of tribulation, then we best start "tribulatin'." That is to say, as Colvin herself does, that when we're under chronic stress we must make time and space to process our emotions and then stay patient with ourselves, allowing our foggy, racing minds to absorb it all—indeed, as Christ urges, resting in and trusting in God's care.

Ancient Christians called this *aequanimitas*. Equanimity. It's that evenness of temper, that sense of composure, that balanced temperament we all want and need in order to face the day well. At the very least, equanimity probably involves first gaining a better understanding about the signals our minds and bodies are sending us. But it also requires us to listen to them. As you pray the prayer below, perhaps picture yourself sitting in the fog in a forest, by a lake, or in a city park. Just rest there until it clears, until it lifts.

> God, help me to slow down, to find a moment of solitude, and to rest my racing mind. In this moment, as I hit the pause button and breathe deeply, bestow on me a glimpse of clarity in my bustling consciousness to identify the fear, the grief, the sadness, the uncertainty that is there, and to just sit with it all for a while. Let me think on it, considering its sources, considering the fleeting nature of it all. God, I now lift all this before you, just holding it all still. Still. Before you. God, work on this with me. Amen.

CHAPTER 23

TAKE A BOW

It was an "off" day. Not as in I took the day off. I was *off-off*. Mentally. Spiritually. Physically. Not myself. I worked, but my to-do list received barely a glancing blow. I forgot my only Zoom meeting of the day. Then, I let myself become irritated by news headlines, yet continued, digital story after digital story, into a veritable doomscroll until I was fully vexed. My exercise was lazy—more a slow trudge than a fleet-footed run. I didn't eat well, and my interactions with family ran the not-so-expansive gamut from unengaged to short-tempered. By the time the sun went down, I was in full "Billy Goat Gruff" mode, according to my wife, and that was all before my favorite baseball team lost.

Based on the day's industry and flow, one often feels a rewarding sense of full-heartedness in the evening—the terrific feeling of earned success that we call "a good day's work." I felt not a hint of it that day. So, in a bit of a funk, I put on some music and listened to a song called "Grace":

> Grace, she takes the blame
> She covers the shame . . .
>
> It's the name for a girl
> It's also a thought that changed the world. . .
>
> And when she walks on the street
> You can hear the strings
> Grace finds goodness in everything. . .
>
> When she goes to work
> You can hear her strings
> Grace finds beauty in everything.[1]

Think of what we've recently endured in the midst of uncertainty and stress. It's simply an unavoidable fact that it will all back up on us some days. It can't be helped. With all that we've been muddling our way through, the fact that we're even upright could be considered reason for taking a bow. It's required wisdom, ingenuity, and tenacity just to get this far. So, in the midst of a busted year, running into a bad personal day, even one beyond the general trouble at hand, should not be surprising. No one performs well every day.

When I misplay one day or even a few, I remember what I used to teach the little leaguers I coached. When a player didn't get his glove down as a grounder approached and thus made an error, I'd tell him to just "brush it off"—literally, to brush his hand over his chest in a motion of whisking it away. The gesture was designed to put the bad play in the past and get refocused for what was next.

It's an often overlooked blessing that our world spins as it does, day to night and back again. We get the chance to brush our poor performances away to a considerable degree because of this. We're given rest and sleep. Through our circadian rhythms, God turns the page for us. The griefs and friction of each day are cut and abridged, put to bed as it were, so they don't pile up as they might otherwise if not for this arrangement. Think about it—what a miracle it is that essentially the lights go out, then reliably the lights come back on again as we regain consciousness each morning and get to start over in a semblance of newness. Scientists can't explain this fully even now. *We just know it is grace at work.*

In addition, Earth is moving around the Sun in an almost circular orbit at a speed of roughly 30 kilometers per second—that's a brisk 67,000 miles per hour if you do the math. That is to say, we're really moving. The confounding trip around the sun we knew as 2020 has passed into memory, and while some of the difficulty and strain that characterized the year reverberates into the next and beyond, we're gaining traction, we're integrating, we're dealing with it, and the calendar will keep turning, bringing with it again and again yet another semblance of the new. That is grace at work too. *Can you hear her strings?*

Finally, it's also by a quiet grace that day by day—even the ones in which we perform especially badly—we're continuing to gather resilience. We're accumulating grit. We're running with weights around our ankles and getting stronger. We're quietly, almost unconsciously, gaining skills all the way through this experience. Quite literally, we're learning to better handle adversity just by getting up every morning. So wherever you are right now, stop and take a bow. A deep one.

God, so I had a bad day. I didn't get my glove down.
Help me to brush it off. To receive grace. To listen for

her strings. And to know that grace finds goodness
and beauty in everything. Amen.

CHAPTER 24

COMFORT. WONDER. SUNLIGHT. FAMILY.

Sunday: Comfort, Texas. 9 pm CST.
The cicadas, crickets, and grasshoppers are clicking, buzzing, and singing, each pushing for evening air time here, running their tiny bows across symphonic bodies like an orchestra warming up before a performance. Only this *is* the performance, one among ancient cypress trees. It's dark now, but I spot a deer in the meadow across the brook. Hank, my opinionated son with whom I am driving to California, insists that it's only a stump. We debate it for ten minutes during which neither my position nor the deer itself has moved. I relent. The final lesson of this Sabbath day is that you can't take pictures of fireflies with an iPhone. God simply makes you enjoy them in the moment.

Monday: Comfort, Texas. 7 am CST.
Growing up, we had plastic place mats on our kitchen table. One had pictures and was called "The Birds of Texas." Well, those birds are all out here this morning, their carols rising with the sun. I hear the rapid knock of a committed woodpecker. I can't tell the direction it's coming from other than "up there," which as directions go is a good one. Near the porch, a hummingbird pivots miraculously over honeysuckle, her wings humming with speed. Next, a yellow finch with a black cowlick arrives, alighting on the railing in front of me. When he departs, I think of the beautiful economy of the word "flit." Above me, a cardinal the exact color of a Stan Musial cap chases a flagrant blue jay around a tall oak tree, which brings three more things to mind: there was another plastic place mat called "The Trees of Texas"; "swoop" is a fine word; and this place is aptly named.

Monday: Outside of Marfa, Texas. 8 pm CST.
Texas is a big, big state, and the wide expanse of the Presidio County landscape emphasizes the miles. That's 357 clicks today. As the sun sets and the night busies itself hanging stars, Hank and I stop at what's irresistibly named the "Marfa Mystery Lights Viewing Area." Here, a plaque tells us that Robert Reed Ellison, a young cowboy, first recorded seeing the mystery

lights in 1883 while tending a herd of cattle. He thought the "ghost lights," which appear in the mountains to the southwest, might be Apache camp-fires except that they kept disappearing, merging, then reappearing. Later theories ranged from the mundane (ranch house lights) to the scientific (the Moon reflecting off mica in the soil), to the science fictive (UFOs or the spirits of dead conquistadors). The lights remain unexplained, yet there they are. Just as amazing as the Marfa lights, though, is the paste of stars above. Though explainable, they remain unbelievable with respect to their numbers, distance, and size. Still more compelling to me, at least tonight, are the sporadic sightings of satellites crossing the night sky at steady veloc-ities. On this extended Sabbath day, I've seen so much of God's wonder that my eyes hurt.

Tuesday: Outside Tucson, Arizona. 107 degrees Fahrenheit.
But it's a dry heat, right? The skies are brilliant cobalt blue and the sun is beating down on us as we make our desert crossing. To the extent that the Coronado National Forest is a forest, it is one composed mainly of enor-mous rocks stacked atop each other, many of them balanced precariously where I assume they've been since the time of Coronado himself. It looks like giants placed them here and no one dared move them. Also, as a bonus today, I used the words *chaparral* and *mesa* in context. I first discovered I liked to write years ago not far from here. The desert compels such things.

Wednesday: Joshua Tree, California. Dusk.
> I want to feel sunlight on my face
> I see that dust cloud disappear without a trace . . .
> I'll show you a place,
> High on the desert plain,
> Where the streets have no name.[1]

Thursday: Los Angeles, California. Redbird Restaurant. 7 pm PST.
My sister Susan lives in Los Angeles. Now Hank does too. I'm glad there's more than one of them here now. We all need backup.

> God, thank you for *Sabbath*. It seems luxurious, a priv-ilege, especially in these times, yet you know what I need more than I do, and you have settled the matter by command. It's my part only to obey and to thank you for the gift. I pray that how I live—mind and body

graced with rest, perspective changed, and soul restored—now blesses you. Might all of us find something like this. Amen.

CHAPTER 25

A HOLY SHRUG

Kelly and I celebrated our twenty-fifth wedding anniversary in Ireland, and, wanting to do something quintessentially Irish while in Dublin, we bought tickets and then attended a show at the Irish National Theatre. We saw *Ulysses*, a play based on James Joyce's novel of the same name. What Mark Twain is to America and what Dickens is to Britain, Joyce is to Ireland. While the play was only a couple of hours long, *Ulysses*, the book, runs over 750 pages, and the reason it's so long is that what Joyce does in his novel is render, in depth and at length, page after page, every thought, feeling, and emotion that his main character, Leopold Bloom, experiences during a single day in the city of Dublin. And while this stream-of-consciousness style of getting inside Bloom's head is what literary critics love about the book, it's also what keeps the book from being more widely read. Page 100 is about as far as I've gotten. And because I've never made it through *Ulysses*, the closest I've ever been to being in inside someone else's head was reading the brief entries in my father's diaries after he passed away a few years ago. Dad had just jotted down a thought or two each day in a little calendar book. Here are a few of the entries:

> *October 7, 1970:* P [that's Pat, my mom] b-day tomorrow. Greg says to get her a robot so we can sit around and drink root beer all day.
> *July 8, 1971:* Pat's folks coming in. When her folks are here, she gets upset with me for no reason.

Skipping ahead a few years:

> *March 3, 1977:* D [my brother, David] had first baseball practice today. Think it's going to be a long season.
> *March 14, 1977:* Greg's team lost again.

Then, after a string of baseball-related entries through April 3:

> Baseball's ruining our lives.

It may not be James Joyce, but by following along day after day, I began to feel the fabric of my father's life, and while there are a lot of funny little things in the diaries, in the more serious and revealing stretches I began to feel his stress over owning his own business, the anxiety he faced about the illness of his own father, and the real concern he had about his growing family's future. And what was both most compelling and endearing was that, the longer I read, the more I heard the words he wrote not in my voice but in his. It was as if I was inside his head hearing his quiet inner dialogue in the midst of the crucial struggles of his life. With the perspective of age (I'm now older than he was when he wrote the entries), I found myself saying, "Dad, don't worry so much. It's going to be OK."

There's this great little slice of the book of Acts in which Paul and Barnabas are in a place called Antioch Pisidia. The gospel is spreading throughout the city. All seems to be going well until the most respected folks in town become convinced that this new way of life on offer to the town's citizens is threatening theirs, and they turn on Paul and Barnabas and force them to leave. Paul and Barnabas, in response, just shrug their shoulders, shake the dust off their feet, and go to the next town, brimming with joy. *An interesting reaction.*

Guy Winch is a licensed psychologist with a PhD from NYU. He's written a book called *Emotional First Aid*, and in it he tells of a young woman who, after twenty years of marriage and an ugly divorce, was ready to date again. She'd met someone online. He seemed earnest and successful. She bought a new dress and they met at an upscale restaurant, but ten minutes into the date he stood up, said, "I'm not interested," and walked out. In need, the woman reached out to a friend, but her friend told her, "Well, what did you expect? You have nothing interesting to say. Why would a handsome, successful man like that ever go out with a loser like you?"[1]

You might, Winch says, ask why a friend would be so cruel. Good question, but Winch says it's much less shocking if we know the truth: *It wasn't a friend who said these things. It was the woman herself.* For that's what we do, isn't it? Especially after a rejection, we begin to focus on all our faults and shortcomings. What we wish we were. What we wish we weren't. And we begin to ruminate about it. It could be said that while some post-disappointment debriefing, some self-analysis, and a bit of self-awareness are always needed, endlessly chewing over one's mistakes and misfortune is too much. Such rumination can easily slide us into a debilitating habit that soon not only compromises our emotional health but also stalls us spiritually, taking us out of the progression of our lives and often out of God's story itself.

Dr. Winch instructs us to combat this, our human tendency toward unhealthy rumination, with just two-minute distractions. When the urge to ruminate arises, a two-minute distraction can begin to break the cycle. *A prayer, a thought sourced in gratitude, a quick break to take your mind in a different direction.* If you know you have the tendency to ruminate over past failures or rejection, this sort of cognitive therapy is a good first step.

We ought to let Paul and Barnabas weigh in on this too because it sounds like they had more than just a positive inner dialogue going on. Despite experiencing a real setback, they didn't get stuck in it. They shrugged it off and moved on with joy. They knew they lived in a heady time, and no matter what unfortunate *local* thing occurred, they knew they were needed in God's larger ongoing story, and that thought energized them. It motivated them. It moved them onward with joy.

You might say that was then, and this is now, and we don't live in such heady times anymore. We live in a time of pandemic, social upheaval, and economic stress. We might be tempted to say that God is not active like that anymore. That was in the first century, and now we're in the twenty-first century—in the modern world. We might ask whether there is any evidence at all that God is still at work as dynamically in our own times, with people like us, as God was in the first century, with people like Paul and Barnabas. What if we were to ask what God's been up to in the world with people like us in, say, the last two hundred years, and especially within our lifetimes, say, in the last twenty-five to thirty years? Let's look at some recent world history.

Start with life itself. Two hundred years ago, nearly 40 percent of children worldwide died before their fifth birthdays. That number has decreased to 6 percent. While we still have a long way to go, this good trend has been accelerating—especially in the last twenty-five years. There's been more than a 50 percent decline in child mortality since 1990, globally. What that means is that 122 million kids' lives have been saved over the past twenty-five years due mainly to the availability of vaccines, access to cleaner water, and better nourishment and education.

What about living conditions? Two hundred years ago, 90 percent of the world's population lived in extreme poverty. Today, fewer than 10 percent of people do.[2] Extreme poverty has been steadily declining over the last twenty-five to thirty years (though that progress admittedly has been halted by the COVID-19 pandemic).[3] But a recent survey revealed that 70 percent of people thought poverty had increased significantly in the last twenty-five years, and only 1 percent knew that extreme poverty had been cut in half over the same period. One and a quarter *billion* people have escaped extreme poverty in the last quarter century, but somehow we've missed it.

There are more good findings. As of 2016, 86 percent of the world's population under the age of twenty-five can read and write.[4] Additionally, the world has never been more democratic than it is now. According to Pew Research, the "share of democracies among the world's governments has been on an upward trend since the mid-1970s," with 57 percent of the world's population currently living in democracies.[5]

While problems facing the world, and our own country, remain enormous, and the trials in front of us remain challenging and even existential, by any reasonable standard we live in a world that is more peaceful, more prosperous, freer, safer, more dynamic, and happier than ever before, and through it all the gospel message has continued to spread. According to a 2015 Pew Research Center survey, by 2050 the worldwide Christian population is expected to be almost 3 billion people—all from the work, the teachings, and the sacrifice of Jesus, his twelve disciples, Paul and Barnabas, the others like them . . . and us.[6]

So the answer is "yes." God is still active in the world, and *these* are heady times, perhaps even more so than in the first century, and God is still using people like us, like you and me, all around the globe. Even now. Especially now. Onward.

> God, may I keep my setbacks and failures in perspective, not with excessive rumination but with joy and, when appropriate, with a holy shrug. Amen.

CHAPTER 26

FIRST THINGS

Amy Herndon passed away a little over two years ago. Amy had a radiant smile, a casual beauty, and unpretentious elegance about her. And, as she battled cancer, she was *Joan of Arc* brave. Amy held newborns in the church nursery on Sundays and taught "Missions" on Wednesday nights with my wife Kelly for many years. Kelly loved being around her, whether they were out at dinner or teaching at church, because Amy was always so disarmingly authentic. She also had an effortless yet striking fashion sense. When Kelly asked her how she put together an outfit, Amy said she just found something she liked, was drawn to, and felt good in, then developed the rest around that. Her biker boots were among her favorite items to build around.

Emily Howard Wilson is another good friend of my wife's, and she is my friend as well. Emily is a designer and has a terrific eye. I asked her not long ago to help me improve the look of my office—to choose colors and help me think about furniture. The first thing she did was walk in and look around a bit. After a minute, her eyes fell on the spine of a particular book among many others on my bookshelf. It was a volume on Jungian symbols given to me as a gift long ago. It had a textured light blue cover with a hint of bronze. She said, "I like that." So that's where we started—with the pleasant color of an interesting book. We matched a paint to the hue of its cover and then had a wall painted in that shade. This led to the purchase of cool gray mid-century–modern chairs and a walnut coffee table, which then led to finding an attractive glass and bronze side table. My office soon became a comfortable, agreeable space to work.

Web designers say the same thing. When you click open a page on your computer, they consider where your eye is likely to go first. A good design has a compelling visual entry point that typically draws the user's attention, and, for one element to stand out, others must fade into the background. Too much going on diminishes the focal point, creating confusion and disharmony. In the realm of fashion, Coco Chanel recommended, "When putting on accessories, take off the last thing you've put on." There's something to be said for not overdoing it.

Sometimes it's exactly what you leave out that makes things work. With respect to editing, Hemingway always urged his writer friends to "kill your darlings." Even if an author loves a passage, if it doesn't move the action, advance the theme, or stir the reader's interest to go on, to go deeper, it probably ought to be excised. Most of the time when you do this, you find that the notion edited out is still somehow there. It remains, in a sense, baked into the whole.

Here's the thing: whether it's fashion, writing, imagining a room, planning a website, or almost anything else, if we want things to cohere, we need a focal point to anchor us and from which to build. And we need to sweep away a lot of what remains. In the same way, each of us benefits from having identified our life's central aim, a worthy ambition to which we then devote our primary, though not exclusive, attention. Choosing that *first thing* is crucial because everything else cascades from that choice.

What is that first thing for you? *Curate your life for a minute.* What do you put on first? What draws and magnetizes your soul? Build and develop the rest around that. As you arise and walk into your day, take a deep breath and look around a bit. Where are you directing your attention today, this week, this month, this season? Name it. Is it your faith? Is it the family God has blessed you with? Is it a project born of the gifts God has given you?

And ask this: What do you need to pare back so that a focal point can emerge more clearly and in fuller relief? Look around. Find that focus. Keep reminding yourself about it and coming back to it, especially in a time when chaos is pushing against the normal order so relentlessly.

What is your *first thing?*

> God, help me to make room for some free space where I can recapture my soul's central point and motivation in the midst of all that's going on. May I find in this space a sense of wholeness, a sense of rightness, and adhere to it rigorously, then adeptly, then . . . *effortlessly.* Amen.

CHAPTER 27

HARPOONERS

Since my boys' little league days have ended, I've missed coaching baseball. Throwing batting practice, hitting infield, the connections with the players and their parents, the excitement of game days in the springtime—I loved it all. I was a decent coach, but the one thing I couldn't ever get the kids to do, even under the scorching Houston sun, was to drink enough water. If you wait until you're thirsty, I'd tell them, it's too late. You're likely already dehydrated and your performance has already started to suffer. The kids never listened, but then again, to tell the truth, neither did I. Unless we're intentional about it, most of us rely on the process of getting thirsty before we drink water.

Not too long ago, I drove to Los Angeles with my oldest son, Hank. As we moved westward across the long, arid landscapes of West Texas, New Mexico, and Arizona, we kept seeing signs along the highway like this: "Next Gas, 100 miles." Even without the helpful reminders, I found myself glancing down at the gas gauge frequently. A trek through the desert tends to focus your mind on the status of your fuel.

As I look ahead at each approaching week and the things I need to do, I typically start searching for when my breaks will be. When am I going to be thirsty for restoration? When am I likely to be running on empty? And I then prudently begin to build in space where I foresee that I can get a breather to replenish my spirit, refuel my body, and rest my mind a bit. I plan it, even calendar it, and then guess what happens? It almost never works out. The "have to dos" invariably expand, crowding out the dili-gently reserved recharging space.

When I first became a minister, I read a book titled *The Contemplative Pastor* by Eugene Peterson. In it, Peterson wrote about a posture, a mindset, a way we might think in the context of better caring for ourselves so that we can better care for one another. Here's the passage:

> In Herman Melville's *Moby Dick*, there's a turbulent scene in which a whaleboat scuds across a frothing ocean in pursuit of the great, white whale. The sailors are laboring fiercely, every muscle taut, all attention and energy concentrated on the task. The cosmic conflict between good and evil joined; chaotic sea and demonic sea monster versus the

morally outraged man, Captain Ahab. In this boat, however, there's one man who does nothing. He doesn't hold an oar; he doesn't perspire; he doesn't shout. He is languid in the crash and the cursing. This man is the harpooner, quiet and poised, waiting. And then there's this sentence: *"To insure the greatest efficiency in the dart, the harpooners of this world must start to their feet out of idleness, and not out of toil."*

. . . In this world, noise is inevitable, and immense energy is expended. But if there is no harpooner in the boat, there will be no proper finish to the chase. Or if the harpooner is exhausted, having abandoned his assignment and become an oarsman, he will not be ready and accurate when it's time to throw his javelin.

Somehow it always seems more compelling to assume the work of the oarsman, laboring mightily in a moral cause, throwing our energy into a fray we know has immortal consequence. . . . There is, though, other important work to do. Someone must throw the dart. Some must be harpooners.[1]

Drink some more water. Refuel your tanks. Be rigid about keeping something in reserve. Sit still, harpoon in hand. Ready. Quiet. Poised. Don't exhaust yourself. At least every once in a while, act out of idleness, not out of toil.

> God, help me to drink before I thirst. To refuel long before nearing "E." To confidently hew to the duty to put down work in the same way that I feel the need to take it up. To realize that my own sense of indispensability is, in almost every case, mythical. To refuse to measure my self-worth by how busy I am. To see that stillness, not speed, best aims the archer's arrow. To placidly take on the poised mindset of the harpooner, rising when needed to meet what's ahead, not out of bustle and toil but in slow contemplation, with a quietly idling mind. Amen.

CHAPTER 28

BEAUTY. AWARENESS. MOMENTUM.

Have there always been this many butterflies, or have I just been missing them? Even in a time of crisis, there is beauty literally flying all around us. The flight demonstration squadron known as the Blue Angels flew over my house not long ago. Remarkable. Can you look up into a sunny sky right now? Or maybe it's raining as you read this. It doesn't matter. Both are beautiful. We can recognize that there is suffering *and* there is beauty all around us. To acknowledge beauty is not to deny suffering.

So take a walk along your favorite trail or in your favorite park. Meet your neighbors across the street under the setting sun. It's almost like Halloween every night; there are so many more people walking around in the neighborhood these days. Listen to all the stirring music at your fingertips, from Bach to the Beach Boys to Bon Iver. We're in a new and golden age of television too, if you know where to look. Compelling stories, well told and meaningful.

Beauty. What's beautiful to you? What out there makes your heart beat faster? What's the most amazing thing about your family, your friends, your city? Name it. What in God's creation lights you up? Call it out when you see it. Explore why this moment, this thing, this sound appeals to you, creates a sense of awe, and makes you feel good. Praise God for it. Follow up on it. This is worship.

Awareness. Rob Jefferies, a member of our church, recently tipped me off to a book written by actor Stephen Tobolowsky (most famous for his portrayal of an insurance salesman named Ned Ryerson in *Groundhog Day*). The book is titled *My Adventures with God*. In it, Stephen tells the story that, at the urging of his rabbi, he began the practice of praying the "Shema" from Deuteronomy 6 ("The LORD is our God; the LORD is one") while on a movie shoot. The rabbi urged him to speak the prayer not only when something went right and he felt blessed but also whenever something *didn't* go wrong (or at least didn't get any worse).

Attuned by this exercise, Tobolowsky began to recognize the appearance of blessing and the avoidance of calamity everywhere. Soon he was saying the prayer so often that he abbreviated the process into just saying the word *Shema*. He continued as the movie shoot wore on, and soon it was *Shema, Shema, Shema* morning, noon, and night. The practice quickly rewired him to see the beauty in his life so frequently that it became perpetual, feeding on its own momentum, renewing his heart and mind in just a short season.[1]

Momentum. When I mentioned Tobolowsky's practice in a sermon, another member of our church, Larissa Fletcher, told me she's tried to incorporate this exercise into her life and that of her daughter, Emma. Emma had ardently taken up the practice, but instead of saying "Shema," Emma simply says the word "Shoe-Mat" when she feels and recognizes blessing.

Attend the beauty flying all around you. Call out both the blessing and the avoidance of calamity you see, signaling your awareness of it to God. Then, feel the flywheel begin to move, creating a transforming momentum that ushers into your soul a new and deeper sense of joy.

"Shoe-Mat!"

> God, Creator of beauty and love, I know and feel the suffering of those all around me. I pray for healing. At the same time, let me not miss the indelible moments of soaring beauty surrounding me now. Help me navigate this tension in a way that dignifies suffering but also recognizes blessing. Bring a new focus to my eyes so that I see all that is the good and beautiful I encounter, but not only this. Sharpen my vision also such that I become more gratefully aware of the bad experiences that are avoided, that are sidestepped, or that could have been worse. May I experience my life with a more sustained sense of joy and added insight, which then prompts me to see even more, including what I missed before. Like all those butterflies. Amen.

CHAPTER 29

SHHHHH

Anders Ericsson was fifteen and loved chess. He routinely trounced his classmates in the cafeteria at school until one boy, the worst player at the school, slowly and methodically became one of its best and took Anders down. Anders knew the kid was practicing a lot, but *how* was this happening? The question lodged in his mind so durably that when Anders went into research later is life, he devoted himself to asking, how do extraordinary achievers *become* extraordinary?

Anders developed an experiment to try to find out. He traveled to a music school in Berlin and divided their violin students into three separate groups: an elite group (each had the potential to be an international soloist); a second group (all good players who would likely play professionally in some capacity later in life); and finally a third group (solid players whose main aim was to direct their passion for music into becoming outstanding teachers). All three groups had almost identical classroom requirements, but Anders, looking for clues, asked all of them to keep journals of their daily routines.

Surprisingly, he found that each group spent about the same amount of time practicing—generally around fifty hours per week. But his research turned up one significant difference in the groups. The first group, the elite group, spent most of their time practicing *in solitude*. They practiced an average of twenty-four and a half hours per week totally by themselves, while the last group practiced on their own only about nine and a half hours per week. In other words, the elite group practiced in solitude well over twice as much as the third group.

If you ask Anders what's so magical about solitude, he'll tell you, just as he told Susan Cain for her terrific book *Quiet*, that only when we are alone can we engage in "deliberate practice."[1] When you practice deliberately in solitude, you strive right into the area of your greatest need, the gap that you know exists in your particular skill set and that you need to grasp in order to improve at that moment. And it's only through undistracted intentionality in solitude that your focused attention is brought to bear specifically on your most difficult ongoing challenge.

Given our world's extreme connectivity, most of us, whether we know it or not, thirst for what comes with solitude. Jesus certainly knew this. He disappeared sometimes. For instance, do you recall what he did when he was told that his cousin, John the Baptist, had been executed by Herod? He withdrew by boat privately to a solitary place (Matt 14:12-13).

With all that's going on around us, solitude is crucial both for grieving our losses during this season and for hearing God guide us in and through our brokenness to a more wholesome and imaginative response to the ongoing experience of tragedy and trouble.

We don't know exactly what Jesus did when he withdrew, but we do know he retreated to be alone. Presumably he prayed. Perhaps he had to regather himself in order to control his anger about the violent injustice that had occurred at the hands of Herod. Maybe he needed to process his own fear, as he surely would have seen John's murder as a foreshadowing of his own coming death. The one thing we know for certain is what Jesus did when he returned from his time away.

When he came back, the Scriptures tell us, the crowds that had heard of John's execution were intent on tracking Jesus down. It seems likely that they wanted to know what they ought to do in response to the injustice of the murder. They were going to take their cues from Jesus. And here's what happened. Having come forth, the gospel story tells us, Jesus saw the vast multitude on shore, some 5,000 people, and that was just counting the men. It was a small army, one ready to take matters into their own hands if told to do so. And the Scripture tells us that Jesus, rather than taking command, rather than inciting the crowd toward revenge, did something completely different. Jesus, *moved with compassion for them*, began to heal their sick (Matt 14:14).

Picture it. What I envision is Jesus' boat coming to shore, crunching to a stop on the beach, facing some 5,000 men and thousands more women and children, some with crude weapons and knives in their hands, a mob ready to do his bidding against Herod in revenge for John's death. Jesus looks around, takes a deep breath, then climbs from the boat and wades to shore where, against all expectations, he says nothing at all to those gathered. Instead he just starts healing people.

Can you see it? He spots a sick child among the bustling crowd on the beach, and, walking past the warriors, he heals her. Maybe she's not much younger than Salome, who danced for Herod at her mother's insistence. Then Jesus heals others, then others. Where most had expected a war, they got love instead. And they begin to drop their crude weapons and their knives on the rocky shoreline as Jesus' disciples come to him, saying, "Teacher, this place is uninhabited and the hour is advanced; we ought to dismiss the crowds." But Jesus is not done. He responds, "No. Give them something to eat." The disciples tell him that they only have five loaves and two fish. And Jesus asks them to bring the loaves and fish forward. He blesses the food and then proceeds to feed *all of them* miraculously with only what they have, filling every person present to complete satisfaction (Matt 14:15-21).

How did the moments of solitude inform what Jesus did? We don't know for sure, but what he did following these moments alone was *completely counterintuitive.* He didn't strike back. He didn't speak about responsibility or assign blame; there was no speech at all. There was just the quiet work of healing and feeding. A miracle from the silence.

> God, it seems like I keep getting bad news, and this season is stretching on too long with the possibility of more trouble ahead. Help me find some solitude to pray, to be quiet into, to rest into, to grieve into, so I can then return, not to speak or blame but to heal and feed. Amen.

CHAPTER 30

SUPERPOWER

If you were told you could have one superpower, what would it be? Just one. According to a website that asked readers this compelling question recently, some of the top desired superpowers are super speed; super strength; flight; time travel; and the ever-popular invisibility. I'd take any of these, but what I think would be interesting is the ability not to be invisible but to *see* the invisible.

What if you could see what God sees? What if you could see God actively working in the world? What if you could watch mercy gather? What if you could observe human pain recede as forgiveness sets in? What if you could clearly behold how generosity and grace change the world? What if you could see how love is bigger and more powerful than anything and everything that can be put in its way?

What if you could see intangible things like unspoken feelings, not to take advantage of them but to help people connect to them, with them, and to each other. What if you could see, for instance, a father's unspoken love for his son, a mother's unexpressed love for her daughter, or our love for one another that we so often can't or don't put it into words despite being given a hundred chances each day to do so. And what if we could see how a mysterious sense of spiritual prosperity often, perhaps even reliably, arises from and through some of the hardest experiences we endure in life?

While we can only see what is tangible and physical before us, God's vision is different. God's economy is different from ours. God sees the invisible. And as I read through the Beatitudes in Jesus' Sermon on the Mount, a field guide for these times, that's what I think he's telling us—that what we don't see is more important than what we do see. Jesus seems to be letting us in on a crucial secret: that there's a whole other realm beyond what is visible to us and that, ultimately, it's what life is all about. It's what existence is all about. Think about the multitude of elusive invisibilities that order our lives: *Innocence. Generosity. Love. Grace. Hospitality. Trust. Sacrifice.* Undeniably, these are all around us. Perhaps if we awoke a little more, we could see them better or at least access them more readily.

Just as the wind is evidenced by the movement of the grass over a fetch of meadow, God's work in the world is evident if we know where to look. Today, fewer than 10 percent of people in the world live in extreme poverty, a decrease from 36 percent in 1990.[1] Extreme poverty has been cut in half over the last twenty-five years. That's a quarter of a billion people. This may be the greatest news in the history of the world, and it's happening right before us. Maybe if we exhibited a bit more concentration, if we attuned our hearts and were patient with the idea, we could behold how generosity and grace change the world. There's been a more than 50 percent decline in child mortality in the last thirty years globally.[2] What that means is that 122 million kids' lives have been saved over that period due mainly to the availability of vaccines, access to cleaner water, better nourishment, and education. Due mainly to philanthropy—that is, generosity.

Is it possible that if we took the long view, we might see the evidence that love is bigger and more powerful than anything and everything that tries to stop it? If I pause a moment and remember my history, I recall Franz Jägerstätter, Maximilian Kolbe, Dietrich Bonhoeffer, Mahatma Gandhi, Martin Luther King Jr., Aung San Suu Kyi, Nelson Mandela, Teresa Bojaxhiu (Mother Teresa), and thousands of other men and women whose names we don't know—yet we sense them all around us on account of the blessings we can count. Author George Eliot expressed this notion this way in her classic novel *Middlemarch*, regarding her heroine Dorothea Brooke:

> But the effect of her being on those around her was incalculably diffusive: for the growing good of the world is partly dependent on un-historic acts; and that things are not so ill with you and me as they might have been, is half owing to the number who lived faithfully a hidden life, and rest in unvisited tombs.[3]

Maybe if we listened and made up our mind to keep listening, we'd pick up on these *diffusive* effects of faithfulness better, seeing the beauty of such good and noble *hidden lives* and sense each other's unspoken feelings more effectively—not to take advantage of them but to help people connect to them and to each other. What if we each took advantage of one of the hundreds of chances that typically pass us by each day and instead used them to speak to those we love?

And finally, what if we could see how a deeply etched sense of spiritual prosperity can mysteriously but somehow reliably arise from and through some of the hardest experiences we go through in life, experiences like the kind we're going through now? What if we could somehow discover that we *do* have at least an inkling of this superpower to see the invisible? What if we were then able to hone it, to use it, and to bless God and others with it?

God, help me realize that you reside in the array of invisibilities all around me, which I could see if I resolved to become more aware, more awake; if I could just remain still and think of things that swirl all about me day by day. I am grateful for the imagination you bestowed upon me, for it is my training in dealing with the invisible. May I use it in your name. Amen.

CHAPTER 31

QUANTUM OF SABBATH

My mother had suffered with early onset dementia for two decades and was bedridden when my father began to show signs of Alzheimer's disease. I had a young family. Charlie was a baby, Hank was a little boy, and Kelly and I both had demanding jobs. I set up a series of appointments for my dad with the same neurologists who were following my mother's condition. We'd leave my mother at home with one caregiver and I'd meet another caregiver with Dad at the doctor's office. After all the terrible tests, his doctor told me what we had feared but already knew: crucial parts of his brain were becoming just as bombed out as my mother's.

At the end of the appointment, which had been pretty clinical in nature, the doctor asked if I'd like to see a counselor. I said sure and prepared myself to gather some additional tips about how my brother, sisters, and I could better provide care for two parents with dementia.

Dad went back to the waiting room with the caregiver, and I met the psychologist alone in an office down the hall. I don't even remember how she started; the whole thing remains a blur. But something was triggered inside me: *grief, sadness, anger, resentment, fear, pity, sorrow, frustration, loss.* They all mixed into a single response, and everything that had been building up for who knows how long poured out in a torrent. Tears, sentence fragments, then apologies and embarrassingly messy sobs—it was not only unlike anything I'd experienced but also unlike anything I thought I was capable of emotionally.

With a little distance now, I recognize that the crazy thing wasn't that I broke down and crashed that day. That was psychologically predictable, healthy, and, though brutally exhausting, good for me. What's inexplicable was that even as I knew I was entering into another season of deep, prolonged stress and grief, I never went back to the counselor. I didn't take a break, change what I was doing, or alter how I was caring for myself. I didn't do anything.

Fast-forward. The crazy thing now isn't that, in the face of all the stress we're under, many of us are just barely holding on; the crazy thing is that we're not hearing the warning signs our bodies and psyches are giving us—or even if we're hearing them, we're not doing anything about them. Writer Anne Lamott says it's a crucial and enduring truth in the modern world that almost everything that's broken will work again if you simply unplug it for a few minutes. This, she says, includes you and me. "Radical self-care," she continues, "is quantum."[1] That is, it doesn't just help you; it helps and positively affects everyone you encounter, offering dividends of grace, patient presence, a surplus of love, and a reserve of creativity. It puts in God's hands a healthier body, a set of hands with more stamina, eyes with sharper vision, ears with superior sensitivity, a renewed mind, and a wiser and more emboldened spirit. *It's quantum.* Conversely, when we fail to unplug and reboot routinely, this too affects everyone we encounter. Again, it's quantum.

Even though we know that this sort of self-care is an inherent part of keeping the imperative that Jesus called the greatest commandment, its importance is often not reflected in our lives even in seasons of stress. It's as if God is saying, "Keep the Sabbath," and we're responding, "But people are counting on me. Look, I'm not saying I'm indispensable, but, well . . . ."

In *The Boys of Summer*, Roger Kahn's terrific book about the Brooklyn Dodgers, there's a chapter devoted to Jackie Robinson. Referring not only to that first year when Robinson broke the color barrier but also to Robinson's talent, personality, charisma, and grit, Kahn wrote, "Jackie Robinson didn't merely play at center stage. He *was* center stage, and wherever he walked, center stage moved with him."[2]

This is probably a good way to picture Jesus' three-year ministry in the Galilee. Wherever he was, center stage moved with him. Paralytics were lowered through roofs, women reached out just to touch his cloak, desperate men came to him and pleaded for him to heal their children. At the height of his ministry, lines of people begging for help must have swarmed with constancy around him all the time, a multitude of voices in his ears, besieging him at every moment of every day. Jesus must have felt the exquisite pressure of having many things to do at once, of being needed always, of being responsible, of being the only one who could help.

My friend Seth Humble, a writer, once told me, quoting one of his favorite writers, "Any writer can cut a bad sentence; it takes a great writer to edit out a good one." Just as it's hard to edit out the good in writing, it's hard to edit out and turn away from the urgent good for a less urgent but ultimately larger purpose. Turning it back to Jesus, Fred Craddock wrote that it takes a person "of extraordinary spiritual discernment . . . [to] turn from the good to the power necessary to resource the good."[3] This is the only thing that explains the many references in the Gospels to large crowds following after Christ, pressing in on him and hindering him from going away, yet he did so anyway. He stepped away for a time when it was necessary.

If Jesus Christ was able to do this, can't we?

> God, I know in my bones that when I refuse Sabbath, rest, and recreation, it's at my own spiritual and physical expense and peril. I know the world's graveyards are filled with people who thought they were indispensable. I won't rob you of what you want of me tomorrow by exhausting myself today. Amen.

CHAPTER 32

ZOOM OUT. WAKE UP. WALK ON.

My wide-eyed enthusiasm for the band U2 is well advertised among those who know me. May these three songs and the notions they're coupled with raise a scaffolding for you to climb out of doldrums if you feel stuck.

Zoom Out. U2's song "Stuck in a Moment You Can't Get Out Of" is written as a dialogue between two friends, one of whom is stuck in depression as serious as it gets (from the album *All That You Can't Leave Behind*, 2001).

> I wasn't jumping, for me it was a fall
> It's a long way down to nothing at all
> You've got stuck in a moment and now you can't get out of it . . .
> (But) It's just a moment, this time will pass.

What I mean by "zoom out" is not that long, awkward process of waving goodbye at the end of a Zoom call but the Stoic practice of dynamically pulling back to a new vantage point. Picture a video game where you switch from your character's point of view on the ground to the bird's-eye view. If you feel stuck, move up, swoop upwards and above. Take a wider, high-altitude view. For instance, take a view of the last two or three years before the present moment through the next two or three years beyond the present moment. Suddenly, the present moment isn't the only thing that matters. Yes, it's a dark moment, a strange, character-building time, but it's just a moment. This time will pass.

Wake Up. It's more a brutal prayer of lamentation than a pop song, but the lyrics of U2's "Wake Up Dead Man" are straight out of Psalm 44 (from the album *Pop*, 1997). There are many ways to climb closer to God, but they all start with honesty. If it feels like your prayers are bouncing off the ceiling, up your honesty game and offer God *all* your heart, *all* your emotions, in *faithful lament.*

> Jesus, Jesus help me. I'm alone in this world.
> Tell me, tell me the story. The one about eternity.

The way it's all gonna be.
Wake up, wake up dead man.

These almost scolding lyrics plead for Jesus to get up and help. Though dripping with doubt, even anger, they're honest like the Psalms, our instruction manual for prayer. I suspect God welcomes more, not less, emotional depth and raw honesty in our prayers.

Walk On. U2's song "Walk On" was dedicated to a human rights activist in Burma and later became an American anthem of sorts after the terrorist attacks of September 11, 2001, when U2 sang it at the *America: A Tribute to Heroes* televised benefit concert just ten days after the attacks (from the album *All That You Can't Leave Behind,* 2000). The song also contains a powerful gospel message encouraging us to persevere as we lean into our faith, which promises that what we can see is not all there is.

> And if the darkness is to keep us apart,
> and if the daylight feels a long way off,
> And if your glass heart should crack,
> and for a second you turn back
> Oh no, be strong,
> Walk on . . .
> You're packing a suitcase for a place none of us has been
> A place that has to be believed to be seen . . .

These lyrical messages are beautiful, drawing us out of the funk we might find ourselves in, but just for a moment let's take the song literally. Just *walk on.* Søren Kierkegaard said, "Above all, do not lose your desire to walk."[1] Here are some other prolific walkers whose "road work" and mileage energized their minds, their bodies, and their souls: Woolf, Dickens, Hemingway, Jobs, Gandhi, Mahler, Beethoven, Wordsworth, Whitman, Yousafzai. Are you stuck? Move around. *Just walk. Then walk some more.* Find a rhythm. Think. Be unreachable for a bit. You're in good company. *Walk on.*

> God, change my vantage point. Turn the dial so I can zoom out for the bigger, wider view. Grant me some altitude.
>
> I feel wrung out, run down, ripped off, and empty. Then I feel efficient, joyful, and surprisingly stable. Then

guilty. Then overly pleased with myself. Sometimes I feel nothing at all. Help me to come to you as I am rather than as some false advertisement of myself. Your grace makes room for my honest soul.

Let sunshine, deep breaths, and the rhythm of my steps fill me with a new buoyancy, a vibrancy, a spark. Animate my mind, my body, and my spirit within the simplicity of a nice walk.

Amen.

CHAPTER 33

A, NOT B

Solomon Asch was a Polish American psychologist who studied the phenomenon of conformity. He devised various experiments to explore the influence of group pressure on behavior. Asch asked his test subjects to look at a single line segment and then to match it in terms of its length with one of two other line segments—*A or B*. The answer would be obvious. The right answer was *A*. But rather than ask the subject test-taker to answer the question by himself or herself, Asch instead brought in four additional "fake" test-takers who were actors and sat them at the table with a proctor along with the actual subject test-taker. Then all five, the real test-taker and the actors, were required to state their answers aloud, but here's the kicker: the first four actor test-takers at the table were asked to answer first. And all of them were not only to give the proctor the wrong answer but also to give the *same* wrong answer aloud. They were all to say "B," leaving the fifth test-taker, the subject of the experiment, to answer last.

Imagine you're the fifth test-taker, fifth in line at the table. All five of you are shown the line segments, and you see the answer is clearly *A*, but you hear four perfectly normal people right beside you go down the row, each of them confidently answering the proctor's question: *B. B. B. B.* Now it's your turn. *What do you do?*

Asch found that on average, about one-third—that is, 32 percent—of the participants placed in this situation went along and conformed with the other four, giving the clearly incorrect majority answer. And what's more, in the post-experiment interviews conducted, the subject participants told Asch that they didn't believe their conforming answer was right; they just went along with the group for fear of being ridiculed or thought peculiar. Even more disturbing, a few of the test-takers said they began to believe the group was correct and they were wrong.[1]

Experimenters like the diabolical Dr. Asch tell us we tend to conform to those around us for two main reasons: first, because we want to fit in with the group, and second, because we begin to doubt ourselves and believe, in our heart of hearts, that maybe the larger group is somehow better informed than we are. Whatever the reason, because we're human we tend to readily leave behind what we feel because of what's going on around us.

We might be doing this right now. We see many people around us who seem to be adjusting to this peculiar and unprecedented season pretty well. Maybe they are. Maybe it only seems that way. But it looks like they've figured it out—that they're making it through quite swimmingly. They've adapted to working at home. They've oriented themselves to semi-isolation. Their kids have figured out home or hybrid schooling with little trouble. They've found a sort of "pandemic rhythm" and even seem to be sort of thriving. All the while, you're feeling like you're at the end of your rope, barely holding on. You're not flourishing. You feel strangely hollow, weirdly absent, all but lost in the present—restless but in need of rest, stuck in the mire, and lost in the haze.

You want to shout, "This isn't working!" Everyone around you seems to be saying with a straight face that the answer is *B*, when obviously it's *A*. Can't they see it's not *B*; it's *A*? Yet, in the end, since everyone else has said *B*, and you don't want to rock the boat or appear to be the only one who's losing it, well, you decide that maybe they're right after all. Just suppress everything—the grief, the disappointment—and get on board. And you hear yourself say *B*.

Maybe consider breaking the spell and expressing, even if it's just to yourself or to a close friend, that you're sad, in mourning, broken, isolated, frustrated, wanting not to feel this way. If you feel it, just say it. It takes courage. But take courage. First, you're likely to have a lot more company than you might think. And second, that company doesn't matter anyway. God hears you.

The remarkable poet Christian Wiman puts it this way: "If God is love, then Christ is love for this one person [*you!*], this one place, this one time-bound and time-ravaged self," *right now.*[2] No one else's circumstances or responses to their circumstances are in play. That is to say, what you're enduring now and how you're enduring it or not enduring it is known intimately by the God who loves you. There's no need to cheer up, get into the spirit, or put on a happy face. If it's *A*, it's *A*. Feel what you feel.

> God, I sense in my eternal soul that you know how I suffer. Give me the courage to say I'm spent when I'm spent. Give me the courage also to reach my hand upward from the mire. To know both that I am not alone in feeling the way I do and that I am not alone at all, for you are with me. Amen.

CHAPTER 34

JOY, A KIND OF STRENGTH

Dr. Rev. Kay Towns is a friend. I coached her son, Davis, in little league. Kay is a licensed professional counselor and a Methodist minister who counsels patients struggling with grief, anxiety, and depression. In a conversation with her recently, she said something so profound that I felt what we all feel when we hear something so obvious and wise that we can't believe we missed it before. Kay said, *"Joy is a kind of strength."*

I've always thought of strength as something that you have to earn. You work out to gain muscle. You study hard to gain intellectual firepower. However, a real accrual of psychological strength—the kind we need to contend with the friction of each day—can be extracted from the joyful episodes or even brief moments of joy we experience. Joy, even when it seems fleeting, is a high-octane fuel that delivers something more durable: spiritual resiliency. Where there is joy, strength is available.

There's an old *Bob Newhart Show* episode where Bob and his former college chum Cliff Murdock (also known as "The Peeper") return to their old school for a football game. Before the game, they're excited to get a bite to eat at one of their favorite campus haunts, a bustling bar and restaurant that served cold beer and delicious sandwiches when they attended the university long ago. But when they arrive, they see that it has now become a dark, dingy, and depressing place. Bob, trying to make the best of it and remembering the hardy old menu from his college days, orders a loaded pastrami sandwich with a large plate of fries, to which the surly man behind the bar responds, *"Sounds great. Where're you gonna get it?"*

On one hand, we could say the same thing about joy. Even if we believe it can transmit strength, when we're stuck in a dark and sometimes depressing season, with the menu of where we can go and what we can do severely curtailed, it's a fair rejoinder to say, "Joy—sounds great. Where're you gonna get it?"

As William James writes in *The Varieties of Religious Experience,* some people are "incapable of imagining the invisible."[1] James goes on to recognize that in some of us faith is natural, but for others of us our temperament is such that doubts weigh heavily if not decisively, making faith difficult. I think the same is true for joy.

Some of us are temperamentally inclined to receive and feel joy more than others. If you're one of these folks who are naturally joyful, thank God for your wiring. Stay optimistic in your bearing. Embrace your moments of joy as they come along. Consider how fortitude gathers inside you when you receive these boosts—how they enable you to keep chugging along and how you're able to deflect away the things that dispirit others. Encourage the rest of us with your secret power. Remind us gently and share with us sensitively those things that light you up, especially if you think they might spark us as well.

For those of us who are less apt to "jump for joy" about joy, consider how to become more self-aware of the moments when you experience a sense of uplift, even if it's mild. It might be a song that drives your mood upwards, a book or show that picks you up, the taste of an exceptional cup of coffee in the morning, a cold glass of water after a good workout, a word of praise your child receives from a teacher or a coach, or something as simple as how the sunlight sharply casts a shadow on the ground. Get inside the moment and sit with it a second. Even if you process it without any extraordinary thrill, breathe in deeply, inhaling the degree of joy that's there like oxygen, then let it metabolize as strength inside you, trusting that it can deliver the recharge you need, moving the needle from "E" toward "F" and storing up a measure of resiliency in your soul.

Too often we look up into a beautiful sky, share a good meal with family, or experience a sense of personal wonder, then feel a bit of satisfaction we might vaguely think of as pleasure, possibly give a nod to God, and behave as if that settled the matter. *It doesn't.* God is putting something on offer to us that we need now more than ever. *Extract strength from joy.* As far as I can tell, it's free.

> God, may I attend the episodic joy that descends upon me. May it be converted into strength inside me so that I may bless you right back in some measure. Amen.

CHAPTER 35

PEACE. PACE. LIMITS.

I don't think of myself as a nervous person, but there are moments these days when I feel a tide of anxiety rising inside me. I've got a lot of questions about the future. I am sure you do as well. What tends to release the pressure valve in my psychology is to remind myself that, as it turns out, not everything depends on me. It's obvious, but it's also easy to forget.

Especially in this season, when our physical movement is restricted, what we control is limited, and our abilities to work and connect are abridged, God gives us a chance to rebalance, offering peace to us if we simply remember this: We can't do *everything*. We can't do everything *perfectly*. And we can't do everything *right now*.

Peace. Pace. Limits.

As we begin to shift our thinking toward a longer view of sustainability in this odd time, think of these words as a mechanism not only to nudge you toward a more durable rhythm for this season but also to point you gently along a path on which you may flourish anew. So, as you prepare to offer your prayer to God, find a quiet spot, relax your mind, and perhaps begin by whispering these three words. Let them settle into your soul, expand your conscious presence of God, and begin to bring a slow healing to your busy, beating heart.

Peace. Pace. Limits.

> God, I relax my grip. I've judged myself by standards set not by you but by a measure that came from somewhere else. I now release all notions of my own indispensability. Instead, I rest in you. Breathe into me your tranquility in this quiet moment. Your grace. Your abundant rest. Let it be.
>
> *Peace. Pace. Limits.*
>
> God, in this stillness, I ask that I may follow you not only in direction and in encounter but also in pace. Not too much. Not too little. Not too fast. Not too slow. May I be *Christ-paced* today. As the sunlight ebbs this day, I shall say to you this evening, "It is night. What has

been done has been done. What has not been done has not been done. Let it be."

Peace. Pace. Limits.

God, as I begin to understand the contours of this time, let me accept with humility my own limits. Refuel me in Sabbaths that I faithfully observe. Guide me to people on whom and to places on which I must lean. And finally, God, may I find in this season a thriving purpose, one that brings me into a full-heartedness of a purer and holier sort than I could have known before. Let it be.

Peace. Pace. Limits.

Amen.

CHAPTER 36

GO TO SLEEP . . . PLEASE

"We're really competing with sleep. . ."
—Reed Hastings, CEO of Netflix (when asked about his company's competition)

About fifty years ago, two doctors at the University of Washington began working with 5,000 patients to research how stressful events affect our health. Through in-depth interviews and deep-dive reviews of medical records, Thomas Holmes and Richard Rahe correlated two things: *elevated stress levels and getting sick.*

Here's how they did it: They identified various stressful life events and then—based on talking to the people who had experienced them—weighted their significance and assigned each stressor a numerical value. The higher the stress level that the event caused in the person, the higher the number. Losing a spouse, for example, was a 100.

Based on correlating the medical records and the scores, they then posited that if your cumulative score was over 300, you were at risk of physical illness. At 150–299, your risk of getting sick was moderate. At less than 150, your risk was only slightly elevated.[1]

The rating scale is called the *Holmes-Rahe Stress Inventory.*[2] You can Google it, take the test, and add up your scores later, but from comparing the stressors named on the list to what we're going through now, I have to estimate that the numbers associated with going through a global pandemic, navigating an economic collapse, and everything else we've faced approaches a 100-point stressor on its own. And it gets worse from there depending on your circumstance. Have you been sick? *Count it.* Has a close family member been sick? Have the circumstances of your employment changed? Have you been laid off? Has there been a major change in your living conditions? A major change in your social activities? *Count it.* A change in school for your kids. *Count it.* It all mounts up. It all adds up. *It all accumulates.* It shouldn't surprise us if our bodies ache, our spirits waver, and our voices crack.

Abraham Heschel was born in 1907. Arrested by the Gestapo in Frankfurt in 1938, he was deported to Poland. His mother was murdered by the Nazis and his sisters died in the death camps. Heschel escaped and immigrated to the United States, where he became a college professor of Jewish Ethics and Mysticism, a rabbi, and a best-selling author. He married a concert pianist, was active in the American civil rights movement, and was a good friend of Dr. Martin Luther King, Jr.

Of the Sabbath, Heschel said, "We must go away from the screech of dissonant days, from the nervousness and fury of acquisitiveness and the betrayal in embezzling [our] own life."[3] He called the Sabbath an armistice, a truce. "The world," Heschel continued, "has already been created and will survive without the help of man."[4] Withdraw from the struggle, he urges us, for a day each week, even a few hours. Accept the truce. Take the draw.

OK, but how? Can we cheat on this Holmes-Rahe test to get our score down somehow? How can we unload some points? How can we reduce our number? I think the most important thing we can do is not something mystical or terribly sophisticated but rather this: simply get some sleep. Our minds are moving a mile a minute to process all we're going through as they absorb the stress and wayfinding we're having to do around the new problems and obstacles of this season. They need a break. It's basic science.

While our lymphatic system removes the waste that the working cells of our bodies create, due to the limited size available inside our craniums, the brain doesn't have a lymphatic system like the one that works for the rest of our bodies. Fortunately, though, we have special cells, called glial cells, that flush cerebral spinal fluid through our brains, clearing away much of the metabolic waste that accumulates in our synapses as our brain cells fire during the busy day. But here's the thing—this cerebral spinal fluid rinse, this "power cleanse," only happens when our brains are in what scientists call "slow wave deep sleep."[5]

In other words, when we're awake and the pistons of the brain are using so much energy, firing at full speed, the brain puts off clearing away the waste, but when we go to sleep and aren't so incredibly busy, the brain uses the crucial downtime to clear things out. Neuroscience research demonstrates that in this overnight housekeeping, important synaptic connections are strengthened while those that are less important fade away. As such, remarkably, idea-processing, thought organization, and memory consolidation are all occurring, in some ways most efficiently, when we're asleep.

Further, scientists are learning the ways our creativity and our ability to come up with novel solutions to complex problems are enormously enhanced by a good night of deep sleep. The developing science seems consistent with a sentiment John Steinbeck expressed: "It is a common experience that a problem difficult at night is resolved in the morning after the committee of sleep has worked on it."[6]

Convene the committee and call the meeting to order tonight.

God, I know communion with your presence is on offer to me in prayer, but I believe also that communion can be had somehow when I'm at rest, asleep. Speak to me in my sleep. I offer it to you. Cleanse my mind, my body, my soul as I rest. Amen.

CHAPTER 37

PRUDENCE & PATIENCE. MERCY & GRACE. FORTITUDE & LOVE.

As we forge ahead further into this unusual season, I've been thinking about the power of words to elevate and encourage us. Here are some good ones. Perhaps say them aloud. Just the sound of these words can give you a real "lift":

Prudence & Patience. Mercy & Grace. Fortitude & Love.

As you offer your prayer to God, let these words wash over you, cleansing your mind and heart. Keep them with you as a comfort to soothe your burdened soul as you continue to find new routines in a new era and as you care for yourself and for others.

Prudence & Patience. Mercy & Grace. Fortitude & Love.

> God, as I seek to be a source of grace for others, I ask for your *grace-giving* for myself. Help me to become more aware of all the emotions I'm feeling and the reasons I'm feeling them. Let me become more intentional about naming, expressing, and speaking what I am feeling before you—all that is in my heart. I commit today that all I am feeling—uncertainty, sadness, disappointment, stress, frustration from a lack of control—shall not be misdirected.
>
> *Prudence & Patience. Mercy & Grace. Fortitude & Love.*
>
> God, as I continue to face the trials of isolation, show me what you want me to see. What do you not want me to miss? What chance is here before me to experience the presence of Christ anew?
>
> *Prudence & Patience. Mercy & Grace. Fortitude & Love.*

God, build a new resilience in me, rekindle my relationships, and renew my appreciation of life. Expand my imagination in Christ.

Prudence & Patience. Mercy & Grace. Fortitude & Love.

God, help me to experience and remember the moments of beauty, joy, and hope that you use to bestow on me strength, endurance, and meaning for today. Spur my continued trust in you.

Prudence & Patience. Mercy & Grace. Fortitude & Love.

Amen.

CHAPTER 38

ELEVATION

In the mid-1800s, a forty-year-old man named Elisha Otis was called upon to convert an abandoned Yonkers, New York, sawmill into a factory that made bed frames. The work required laborers to walk up and down multiple staircases many times a day. Otis, an inveterate tinkerer and innovative thinker, designed something he called a "safety elevator" that had a special braking mechanism on it to prevent the hoisted platform it raised from falling to the ground, even if its rope or cable broke. With the help of his sons, he began manufacturing the device commercially, but neither building owners nor the general public yet trusted his invention.

Enter noted American entrepreneur and showman P. T. Barnum, who, in conjunction with his persevering friend Otis, hatched an idea for a public demonstration of the "safety elevator" at the World's Fair held within the Crystal Palace in New York City in May 1854. Under Barnum's orchestration, Otis boarded an open elevator platform installed at the center of the exposition hall. After the elevator was hoisted high above the crowd, Otis called out for a man stationed along a catwalk in the rafters to slash the elevator's cable with a large ax.

As the blade was raised and then swung, horrified onlookers watched, fully expecting the elevator with its foolishly intrepid passenger to plummet under the command of gravity and hit the floor of the hall. Dramatically, though, Otis's safety brake suddenly and stubbornly bit, and the elevator came to an abrupt halt, having fallen less than a foot. The presentation was a sensation, and within two years, Otis had sold twenty-seven elevators with his patented safety brake.

Before 1850 there were almost no buildings over six stories tall. Over the next generation, with the advent of this invention, coupled with the introduction of steel frame construction, dozens of tall, sky-scraping buildings began to rise all over the world.[1]

Travel high above the ground is now something we do with regularity, but if we think about it, our routine ascension into the sky is a sort of miracle. Physically, we have the privilege of routinely seeing things from a lofty perspective that people before the time of Elisha Otis could scarcely imagine. To look out from the top floor of a towering skyscraper, to consider a great metropolitan vista from above, pulls us away psychologically from the myopia of our own lives to see things in a new way. Angles of light are perceived differently. Locations, direction, and connections below can all be seen from on high with enormous clarity, new order, and superior comprehension. There's a majesty in distance and a simple wonder in "the afar."

As it is in the physical world, so it is in the spiritual. In an extraordinary way, we have a similar opportunity to arise routinely, to elevate ourselves on a weekly basis, within the transformative experience of worship each Sunday. This means of ascension is a sort of miracle as well. However, just like we take for granted rising high above the ground by elevator, we often take for granted our opportunity to find elevation through worship.

What if, just as we would look down from an ultra-elevated position of the highest building around, we were to expand our perspective when we're approaching God in worship? If we did this, is it possible that we would gather a more comprehensive picture of our lives in terms of our location in the world and the direction we are moving? Is it possible that with such perspective, we would perceive a wider array of relational connections around us and see them with new clarity and a new sense of order?

One last thing about perspective: they say sometimes a rest is as good as a change, and that may be true, but sometimes only a real change will do. One of the most stubborn challenges of this time has been the travel restrictions. Vacations have been canceled or at least abridged, but even a short weekend day trip, a long walk in the park during the workday, or some other sort of deliberately arranged change in perspective might do the trick. Find a new place in the town or city you're in. Maybe get on Elisha Otis's invention and be lifted up to a high place. *Elevate.* Look around. There's a majesty in distance and a simple wonder in "the afar."

> God, help me to care for myself by finding a new perspective—a place, even if for a short time, that changes the angle of my vision, provides a new way of seeing the dilemmas of the present day, and gives me an original orientation from which hope can be glimpsed and grasped. Amen.

CHAPTER 39

IN LIMINAL SPACE

Johannes Vermeer is most well known for his beautiful painting, *Girl with a Pearl Earring*, but he painted another called *Girl Asleep at a Table*, which can be seen at the Metropolitan Museum of Art in New York. It's kind of odd. A young woman is sitting in a chair at a table off to one side of the canvas, dozing on her hand, her elbow on the table. Also on the table is a large overturned drinking glass. And nearer the girl is a more delicate, upright wine glass. Behind her is an open door, and through the door is a small side table against the far wall, part of a window, and a mirror above the table. The painting is dark and yet still somehow full of deep, rich colors, but it's hard to know what to make of it.

At the Met, they've done X-rays of the painting that show there was originally a man standing in the doorway. Vermeer later apparently decided to paint him out and just left the empty space in the open door. With the man in the doorway, we have one painting. With just the young woman alone, we have a whole different painting. The one we see has a quiet, pensive quality. There's something gloomy about it, even as it remains vague in terms of meaning—just a girl dreaming of something at a table where something has just happened, and we don't know what. We're left to speculate on all of it.

When we lose someone—a person, an item, an expectation—we have to acknowledge that we're in a different painting than we were in before, and the new picture might remain fuzzy, dark, dreamy, vague, and unclear for a time, spinning out feelings of disappointment and sadness as we try to forge ahead into what's next. And here's the thing about feelings: *you have to feel them even if you're not sure what they are.*

When you find yourself in this liminal space, this in-between, this middle place, trying to figure out those feelings and the contours of the new story you're in, be patient as the new picture begins to come to light.

If you're a singer or a musician, or even someone like me who was barely able to hang in there for a couple of years of junior high band, you certainly know what a *fermata* is. It's the mark that looks like a bird's eye and tells you to hold a note out for an unspecified length of time—a length to be determined by the conductor standing at the front. I thought of fermatas as being placed over musical notes exclusively, but recently I learned that composers sometimes put fermatas over rests as well. Beethoven often did this. In some of his most famous sonatas, many of the movements end with a fermata over the final rest. With this notation, Beethoven created an extended period of silence between the movements of music. How long a fermata is held over a rest depends on a lot of factors, but most music people agree it should be held until a reframing occurs. That is, the silence should continue to abide until what the listener just heard settles into her soul, is absorbed meaningfully, and she is now more "experientially" prepared for what's coming next.

If this season has left you not sure about tomorrow, about what's next, or unsure of what your story, your painting, ought to look like now, then hold the fermata, claim this liminal space, this in-between time, this moment simply as a rest between movements in your life.

Jesus quoted one book of the Old Testament more than any other, which indicates that he must have studied it at length. It's the book of Deuteronomy, one we don't study or even peruse much now because it seems so dense with regulations and pointless wanderings. But there are some great stories in there as well. Perhaps the most memorable is a powerful moment near the end of the book, when Moses places the people he's led for over a generation under the care of his successor, Joshua. Moses says to Joshua:

> Be strong. Take courage. You will enter the land with this people, this land that God promised their ancestors. You will make them the proud possessors of it. God is striding ahead of you. He's right there with you. He won't let you down. He won't leave you. Don't be intimidated. Don't worry. (Deut 31:7-8, *The Message*)

It's a recurring motif in these first few books of the Bible—God going out ahead of the people. It's one that, for me, brings to mind the picture of a mother with her child at the threshold of a dark room, the child hesitant and frightened to go in. The mother says, "I'll go in ahead of you and make sure it's safe." But what's most interesting and compelling to me about these words of Moses is not the "striding ahead" but the next line about God being right there with us. It prompts us to ask how God can be both striding into our unknown future ahead of us *and* also right with us in this current liminal space.

I don't know, but I do know that *God can do things like this.*

God, calm my mind and heart in this liminal space. Help me be patient as the future forms from the present darkness. Stride ahead of me, but also don't leave me. I don't know how you do both of these at the same time, but I'm thankful for it. Amen.

CHAPTER 40

CONTENDERS

The futility of trying to map out our future in too much granular detail is captured in former heavyweight boxing champion Mike Tyson's famous adage, *"Everyone has a plan until they get punched in the mouth."* Given that this season has certainly been a real punch in the mouth, maybe it's a good time to look ahead and ask how we roll with the punches and better develop the skills needed to contend with a world of uncertainty and the ongoing blows we must absorb.

Philip Tetlock and Dan Gardner, in their book *Superforecasting: The Art and Science of Prediction*, remind us that although life is made up of unpredictable events, ebbs and flows, and often undetectable cause-and-effect relationships, we're not merely helpless riders on the tides of fate.[1] No, they tell us, life is not a wholly inscrutable mystery. When our forecast horizon is short as it is right now, they urge us, rather than making plans or trying *to dictate the future*, to simply hone new and critical skills of agility, adaptability, and resilience *to deal with it*.

Searching for Bobby Fischer is one of my favorite movies.[2] The film tells the true story of Josh Waitzkin, who was eight years old when, on his way to play on the monkey bars in New York City's Washington Square Park, he saw some men playing chess. He asked if he could play. Once at the table, Josh began showing signs that he was a prodigy. Josh's dad soon signed him up with a chess instructor (played by Ben Kingsley in the movie), who encouraged Josh, in the midst of his matches, to picture an empty chessboard in order to clear his *inner vision* and more adeptly imagine his opponent's options in conjunction with his own moves ahead. Josh, who had played largely instinctually before this, began to mindfully imagine the game forming and developing on the board. In the film, Ben Kingsley's character instructs Josh to consider a dozen or more moves ahead until he can envision the winning path. "Don't move until you see it," he tells Josh. "Don't move until you see it."

We might also consider the wisdom of Calvin Coolidge. President Coolidge, who when faced with a dilemma famously never took "doing nothing" off the table too quickly, provides us with this sage advice: "[I]f you see ten troubles coming down the road, you can be sure that nine will run into the ditch before they reach you and you have to battle with only one of them."[3] Even in the midst of a year of rolling boulders, this sound counsel directs us away from imagining the worst and "catastrophizing" ourselves into paralysis and encourages us toward waiting calmly, keeping an eye on things until acting is necessary.

Within the Sermon on the Mount, following a series of beautiful phrases concerning birds that neither sow nor reap and flowers that neither labor nor spin, Jesus urges us to slow our own motion and not worry so much about our lives and our needs, because God loves us. "Seek ye first the kingdom of God," he tells us (Matt 6:33). Focus on that. Set your mind on it, and then all these other things will be added unto you.

As you forge ahead, stay patient. Refuse to catastrophize about tomorrow. Clear your inner vision so that you might see the kingdom of God forming, developing, prevailing ahead. It is. You can count on that. Then, with this mindset, even though you still may not be able to *see* the future, you'll have developed the aptitude you need to deal with it. Roll with the punches. Don't leap too fast. Let the boulders roll a bit more. Let the ball travel. Let the game come to you, and don't move until you see it.

> God, help me to think about uncertainty not as a threat but as an opportunity to strengthen my trust in you. Help me to consider the blows absorbed during this season not as injuries but as lessons that have produced a better disciple, one who can roll with the punches, one skilled in all the ways of contending. Amen.

SELF-GIVING

"For whoever wants to save their life will lose it, but whoever loses their life for me will find it." —Matthew 16:25

CHAPTER 41

GRACE. LOVE. AND MORE GRACE.

So I'm trying to read *Moby Dick*. Let me just say, it's not going well. I'm stalled on the *Pequod* with Ishmael, Starbuck, and Captain Ahab somewhere in the South Pacific around page 243. I made it through Melville's all but exhaustive description of the Nantucket whaling industry but then bogged down in a chapter called "The Whiteness of the Whale." The book is dull and tedious but also incredibly engrossing, playful, brilliant, funny, and then dull again. It's a tremendous work, but really, really dense.

Maybe I'm being overly ambitious, but I want to be the type of person who's read *Moby Dick*. And *War and Peace*, *Crime and Punishment*, and *Middlemarch* (which I'm also taking a crack at, albeit on Audible—*also not going well*). But it's not just this. It's not just a question of books where there's a gap between who I am and who I want to be. No. My under-achieving extends well beyond literature.

I'm also not the parent I want to be. Nor the husband I want to be. Nor the minister I want to be. I've got issues with openness. I'm not as generous, kind, patient, or faithful to God as I ought to be. I'm prone to grumbling and criticizing. You see, I have this terrific picture of who I want to be, this person I desire to see myself as being, but let's face it: it's not me. It's like having a song in your head that you can't quite sing. And with the added pressure of a pandemic, a quasi-quarantine, and an iffy future, sometimes I can't even find the tune at all.

Scientists from Johns Hopkins recently conducted research in which they compared experiences between those who reported "God encounters" naturally and those who reported such encounters after the use of psychedelic drugs; 809 people responded to the non-drug survey, and 3,476 people responded to the psychedelics survey. After carefully screening the participants, the researchers asked each of them a series of questions from something they called a Mystical Experience Questionnaire. When the 809 participants who reported naturally occurring "God encounters" were asked about the main attributes of the *Being* they experienced, they used the words Benevolent/Compassionate (86 percent), Sacred (81 percent) Eternal (70 percent), and All-Knowing (66 percent).[1] In this research, as well as anecdotally, an overwhelming majority of people who have experienced such mystical encounters typically describe the moment as joyful, one of awe, and they say that, in God's presence, what they sense mainly is the feeling of kindness, acceptance, and transcendent love.[2]

Most of us probably won't ever experience a mystical God encounter of this direct sort, but our faith teaches us that we can encounter, come to know, and gain a deeper access into this transcendent kind of love in a more mundane but just as sacred way—by not just knowing but also internalizing the teachings of Jesus.

In late May every year, I pick up a book called *If This Isn't Nice, What Is?*[3] It's a collection of the commencement addresses of the late author, Kurt Vonnegut. In it, Vonnegut, though famously an atheist, writes that the one good idea humanity has come up with so far is the idea of mercy and grace that Jesus gave us in the Sermon on the Mount.[4] The whole message conveyed in Christ's teachings and then brought to life in his crucifixion and resurrection is that God is just this: *Grace. Love. And more grace.*

Maybe you too have some projects that haven't panned out in this season. Maybe, as you're feeling the stress we're all facing, you feel disinclined to go easy on yourself. Maybe you're beating yourself up for not being the person you think you ought to be or plausibly could be. Keep working on it. The book's not finished yet. But here's how it ends: *Grace. Love. And more grace.*

> God, when my reach exceeds my grasp, help me to remember that your eyes are filled with grace for me. *Grace. Love. And more grace.* Build up my soul with a spiritual confidence not sourced in me, but sourced in you and your bright and inexhaustible love. *Grace. Love. And more grace.* Help me to embody the teachings of Christ. And to never grow weary of going easy on all the people I encounter, becoming a friend, being a neighbor, and being a servant to "the least of these" (Matt 25:40). *Grace. Love. And more grace.* Amen.

CHAPTER 42

"AND THERE WAS LIGHT"

We live in a wild and woolly world. We are reminded of that almost constantly these days. Overlay a pre-2020 world already stressed with high-tech change and postmodern psychic insecurity with a worldwide global pandemic, then stretch our part of the planet thin with a long-time-coming reckoning borne of historic racial inequity, then dice it up further with almost unprecedented political polarization, and it seems we rise in the morning and fall asleep at night just trying to slow down the spinning. Sometimes it feels like we're looking out over the dark icy waters from the vast deck of a large and famous 1900-era oceangoing vessel, scrambling, pointing, shouting, *"Iceberg!"* But no one's listening, and certainly no one's turning the wheel.

> In the beginning God created the heaven and the earth, and the earth was without form and void; and darkness was upon the face of the deep.

The morning after the waters receded following Tropical Storm Harvey, which inundated my hometown of Houston, Texas, not too long ago, I went to the NRG Center adjacent to Houston's NRG Stadium. It was ground zero for the recovery effort. And it was chaos, but not a high-velocity chaos—a slow-moving one. After waiting three hours in line to offer help but doing nothing, I was finally assigned to a volunteer team charged with organizing clothes and supplies that were beginning to come in for survivors who had lost their homes and possessions. Our team, my team, was made up of just me and four or five other people. We were taken to an enormous room, a space the size of an airplane hangar. At the far end of the room were big bay doors open to a dock where folks were coming in and out with loads and loads of clothes and supplies. With respect to our task and with respect to our team, there wasn't anyone in charge as far as I could tell. We were kind of at a loss as to what to do.

Then people from the dock started to bring clothes and stuff in, just dumping it all into a single giant pile in the middle of the room. The pile soon became a little mountain, then a big mountain some twenty feet high in the center of the hangar. Every once in a while, a couple of people with official-looking badges would enter, and they'd point here and there and then leave. I wanted to ask the question, "How do you want us to organize all this? What do you want us to do?" But by the time I could approach them, they would be talking to someone else, then disappear in a hurry. Meanwhile the twenty-foot mountain continued to grow, becoming an impressive mountain range. Essentially, the answer to my question, "What should we be doing?" was echoing through the cavernous room, and the answer, unspoken, seemed to be this: "I don't know exactly, but just start."

So, with the others there, I started separating pants from shirts, shoes from coats, blankets from dresses. Kids' clothes from adults' clothes. Girls' clothes from boys' clothes. Men's clothes from women's clothes. After a couple of hours of this, someone who seemed "sort of in charge" asked me if we needed help. I looked at the still growing pile and then back at the person. "Uh-huh."

Soon twenty-five more people arrived, then fifty. Suddenly, the mountain range was diminishing. Slowly but quite visibly, we were chipping away at it. Then more people came to help. Eventually, people began not just sorting clothes but sorting themselves into tasks. The mountain had disappeared. Piles had turned to stacks and stacks to rows, tables were set up, things were set out by size, by age, and even by color. The people who were strong carried stuff. The people who were good organizers organized. The people who were good administrators administrated. The encouragers encouraged. Ropes were set up to accommodate lines. And by that after- noon, bewildered people who had lost everything, after being been fed and being provided a moment to rest, were ushered into our room and quietly, sacredly even, began to find the things each of them needed most.

> And the Spirit of God moved upon the face of the waters. And God said,
> Let there be light: and there was light.

It's the business of God to speak light into darkness, order into chaos. We tell this ancient story of the Creation not because we know exactly what happened at that moment but because this is the sort of thing that always happens. That's what Genesis is—both the good and the bad. It's what always happens.

Even now, order and chaos vie with each other all around us. The icebergs are still out there. Catastrophe comes, but from it—where people of goodwill show love and exhibit grace to one another—lifeboats appear, chaos is beaten back slowly, and restoration and rebirth emerge. Consider for a moment the glimpses of new life you've witnessed even in this season of dysfunction and sorrow we've been through and are still wading through. A quick joke on a Zoom call. A chalked "we miss you" from your church on your driveway. A note of encouragement from a friend. A call or text from family. Maybe you were the jokester, the chalker, the note-writer, the texter, the caller. Maybe you were on the receiving end.

Keep doing those things and keep thinking up new ones. And keep receiving grace too. Even after this period begins to ebb, and even after it's all over, keep beating the chaos of other messes back with love and mercy. Keep chipping away at that mountain of chaos. If it keeps piling up, don't add to it. Get some more people. We are not victims who are weak; we are resilient survivors, brave and strong. We are people of goodwill, expressing love in acts, in words, in a hundred different ways. We are God's agents.

God said, "Let there be light." And there was light.

> God, let me be one who chips away at the chaos, not one who adds to it. Let me be a little light joined with others, brave and strong, patient, believing that this always happens, but so does Rebirth. Restoration. Resurrection. Hope is ushered in. Amen.

CHAPTER 43

SLANT

Emily Dickinson didn't become known, much less famous as a poet, until well after her death. Dickinson asked her sister Lavinia to burn her papers when she died, but instead, when Emily passed away, Lavinia found her sister's poems and took them to a publisher. If she had not, we would certainly never have heard of Emily Dickinson and never known about her remarkable gem-like poems and the worlds of beauty and wisdom inside each one of them.

Poems like this one:

> Tell all the truth but tell it slant—
> Success in Circuit lies
> Too bright for our infirm Delight
> The Truth's superb surprise
> As Lightning to the Children eased
> With explanation kind
> The Truth must dazzle gradually
> Or every man be blind—[1]

Dickinson is suggesting that sometimes truth is a hard thing to take in. To adhere to the truth, to advocate the truth, and to showcase the truth in our words and actions are all important things to do. But if we wish to *persuade* someone toward the truth, there's more to it. There has to be some thought, some strategy involved. The poet posits that there's an *art* to persuasion. It's something that requires more craft, more patience, more wisdom, more grace, more delicacy than force. It's obviously become something of a lost art.

Dickinson says that we must unfold what we see as truth and want others to believe more slowly, "in circuit," conversationally, disarmingly, winsomely, not so assertively but rather "with explanation kind." Unless we do this, she says, our audience may be left blind, without a deep sense of understanding of our contentions or, worse yet, left angry and resentful because of our overly strident assertions. We must come at it *slant*.

In social psychology, there's something called "the boomerang effect." It refers to the unintended consequences of attempting to forcefully persuade another person of something, which often results not in changing that person's mind but in hardening their opposing position instead. Author Arthur Brooks writes in his book *Love Your Enemies* that when there's too much argumentative punch in our engagements, and especially when there's contempt involved or condescension in our tone, and not enough persuasive "circuitry," we're three times more likely to strengthen an opponent's opposing views rather than to persuade them of the truth of our own. "Almost no one's ever been insulted into agreement," Brooks writes.[2]

If we have a strong view on a matter of faith or a matter of public controversy and wish to advocate for it, perhaps the first question to ask ourselves is, *What is our objective?* Is it to exile or harm the other person? Hopefully not. Is it to demonstrate an opponent's lack of intelligence or hypocrisy? Good luck with that approach. Is it to receive a pat on the back from the like-minded even as we push the other side away? Once again, hopefully not. I could go on, but let's cut to the chase: isn't the goal to make the other person think differently? If so, then ask yourself, *How does one most effectively do this?*

Dickinson suggests a form of persuasion akin to explaining the phenomenon of lightning to the young. Of course, one would tell a child about the strange flashing lights and the terrible rumbles in the sky accompanying a storm in a way that would ease their souls and engender curiosity, exploration, questions, and wonder.

When faced with a legalistic lawyer who had a skeptical view regarding whom his neighbor was, Jesus unspooled the slowly dazzling story of the good Samaritan (Luke 10:25-37). Later, confronted with a host of ornery scholars accusing him of consorting with the wrong sort of folks, Jesus responded obliquely, laying out a series of three superb images—a shepherd going after a lost sheep, a woman who turns her house upside down looking for a missing coin, and a father with a prodigal son (Luke 15). Finally, on his last night in their company, in the moment when he wanted to persuade his closest friends of the truth of who he really was, what his life was about, and what they should do next, Jesus didn't even use words at all. Rather, he used a living metaphor. He acted out the truth like this:

> . . . he got up from the meal, took off his outer clothing, and wrapped a towel around his waist. After that, he poured water into a basin and began to wash his disciples' feet, drying them with the towel that was wrapped around him. (John 13: 4-5)

Do you want to persuade someone, a friend or even an enemy, of the truth? Tell it slant. *Or maybe just wash their feet.*

> God, help me to choose the nuanced art of persuasion, leaning into patience, wisdom, and sensitivity over condescension, assertion, and contempt. Let me embrace truth with more and more of the posture of a graceful servant rather than an indignant advocate. Amen.

CHAPTER 44

MUSIC. MEANING. FRIENDSHIP.

Not long ago, I joined three of my friends—Mark Jones, Brook Ballard, and Jake McKim—to take part in what's called the "30-Day Song Challenge." The experience was something that elevated my soul through some pretty blurry days. Brook is a gifted self-taught harmonica player. Jake founded a talent development group that steers behind-the-scenes strategies for artists like Beyoncé, and Mark's knowledge of music is marrow deep and spiritual in nature. I'm sort of like the guy they allowed into the band because I own a good amp.

Anyway, here's how the challenge worked: each day you're asked to identify your favorite "song with a color in the title" or "song you never get tired of," etc. Things like that. Thirty days, thirty categories. Each morning, you text the group a link or a YouTube clip of the song you've chosen. It was a heartening exercise each day. Both the shared experience and the music itself have quickly became a happy bulwark against all the struggles of a difficult season, but I noticed that as the challenge advanced, it crept into a more personal realm—"a song that you remember from your childhood" or "a song that breaks your heart." It asks for some vulnerability.

Music. Given the remarkable company I kept with these guys, the exercise introduced me to an absorbing soundtrack of previously unknown songs and reintroduced me to artists I'd underappreciated for years. But what was most profound was the sometimes comical, often poignant glimpses I received into my friends' unique personalities. The stories about why particular songs were meaningful to them was the most life-giving and soul-refreshing part of the whole experience.

Meaning. Scripture assures us that where two or more are gathered, God is there, and it turns out that this is true. Sharing almost any experience among friends with a measure of faith and a dose of vulnerability does summon us into God's presence. Add music to this mix, and the separation between the physical world and the spiritual further dissolves. If the music is good enough, the gulf between an ineffable heaven and a gritty dry-seasoned earth sometimes even seems to disappear. It's something akin to a miracle.

Friendship. Isolation is the challenge right now, and human connection is the provision God gives us to overcome it. Music is a gift. You probably have a cool phone. Send a song or two to a friend and see what happens.

After you "Amen" the prayer below, you'll find a link to a Spotify playlist curated by Mark, Brook, Jake, and me. You can call these secular songs, but that's probably missing the point. This music is the work of broken, imperfect folks, but that description also fits a group of Galilean fisherman, a tax collector, and several other equally salty characters who threw in their lot with a carpenter's son some time ago, not to mention a lot of us. *Give it a listen.* There is gospel within U2's lyrics and in the modern-day poetry of the Waterboys. Don't miss it. It's in the jubilation of *Oh Happy Day,* in the youthful exuberance of INXS, in Stevie Wonder's fingers, and in Katy Perry's roaring pop anthem. It shows up in Ike and Tina's jam, in the twang of Ray Davies's guitar, and in Emmy Lou Harris's astonishing voice. It's in the miraculous beauty that somehow routinely emerged from Lennon and McCartney, and it's in Randy Travis's country western confession. Christ shows up where you least expect it. He tends to do that. *Listen up.*

God, what a wonder it is that a series of tones, rhymes, and recurring patterns conduct your life into mine as if through a copper wire dropped from the clouds. And it's a blessing that urges me to engage with friends. In the gift of music I hear echoes, see signs, and sense the awe and truth of your mystery, majesty, power, and grace. In friendship and in these songs and in how they mix together, there is an arresting combination, and I'm grateful for it. Whether in this or in some other facsimile of eternity that you have planted in my heart, broadcast yourself through my peculiar, un-repeatable story, this thing made of years and grace and love, this thing I call "myself," which rests in your hands. Amen.

Our Spotify playlist: https://open.spotify.com/playlist/ 1RZmOVMwVmVIKtQxCyp5nS?si=Mcc-TLu5RK mYZ2IsHvzpcw

CHAPTER 45

RAISING OUR HANDS

My prayers reside especially with the parents of young children who are forging through this strange time with extraordinary patience and innovative thinking regarding their children's education. As I recently considered the challenges of school in this season, I was struck with a nostalgic thought. What if, as a student, I'd had the wherewithal simply to ask more questions, to engage with my teachers more fully, and to embrace the opportunity to dialogue with them as a curious and fearless kid? Back then, when my math teacher asked if the class understood how a particular equation was worked out, and I didn't quite "get" it, I would never raise my hand to confess that I was flummoxed by the concept. In retrospect, I have a feeling that I wasn't the only one. I wish I'd been a bolder, more confident, and more honest student. Maybe there's still a chance for this.

While the sort of pain and tragedy we're chiseling our way through right now can be traced back, to some degree, to various human mistakes and hubris, I feel obliged to raise my hand and say, "I still don't get it. Why is all this happening?"

Genesis, Eden, Adam, Eve, apple, serpent—they all shed some light on the matter of suffering for us. However, notions of free will, sin, and brokenness don't explain everything. There are storms. Injustice is diffused throughout the world and history in a way that often bears little resemblance to what we conceptually think of as fair. The most vulnerable seem to get hurt worst—kids are abused; the oppressed are hated; the aged die alone; the innocent suffer. That's all to say that I think there's still a lot of explaining to do. Maybe you feel like raising your hand right now too.

Since I'm a minister, people ask me about this sort of thing and I'm expected to give a good answer. What I usually encourage folks to do is bring their deepest lamentations, their rawest emotion, their most unvarnished honesty, and their hardest questions directly to God. And while I still think this is good advice—and it is sourced in Scripture, the Psalms in particular—I admit it sometimes sounds hollow, as if I'm saying, well, just pray about it super hard. That's not what I mean, though, so let's try this:

We often think, consciously or subconsciously, that God's presence is announced in our lives based on our circumstances—in the lack of difficulty in our days; in our prosperity; in smooth seas all around. What undergirds this mostly errant thought is the human desire to feel like we're in control, to believe that our obedience, goodness, and faith will somehow slip us karmically, contractually, into a successful and relatively trouble-free life. But this transactional notion is grounded more in the tenets of the insurance industry than in real life. What's worse, it carries a mean whiplash, as when trouble arises, we begin intuitively to think a bad thing has happened because we didn't exhibit enough faith. We would never quite put it this way, but there's something in the back of our heads pinging away a false message: if all is going well, God must be thinking, "I'm pleased with you," but if things are not going well, God must be thinking, "I'm pulling up my stakes to move on to someone who has their life together."

Christian Scharen is an author who writes about something called *the theology of the cross*. In his book *One Step Closer*, he posits that the cross tells us that God tends to show up in the world and in our lives not typically in power, glory, prosperity, strength, and triumph—not from the sky, as it were—but in all that is symbolized in the cross, from the ground in a sense: in loss, in sorrow, in the rubble, and in the complicated, storm-driven moments like the one we're working through right now.[1] The cross readily acknowledges the yawning gap between how things are and how things are "supposed to be." It embraces the dissonance of history and hope, encouraging us toward that raw honesty and authenticity we all yearn for in our relationship not only with God but also with each other.

When I raise my hand and ask God about suffering, what rings back to me as true is this: God's most sacred work is usually hidden in the crosses we carry, and often God's voice arises mysteriously in the midst of the clouds. And the resonant force of this notion leads me to this conviction: I believe with all my heart that God is with you and me, in this time, in this place, in this storm, even now.

> God, I spurn the platitudes I often reach for in the midst of travail. Instead, I raise my hand to reveal to you my questions and my deepest inner struggles. I pray *the cross* would shape and frame how I interpret all that is before me. Help me to embrace the dissonance between my experience in this season and the hope my faith teaches so that I may see your work and find my part in it. I raise my hand. I raise my hand to find it. Amen.

CHAPTER 46

SCOUT

When I was little, I remember watching the film *To Kill a Mockingbird* with my parents. I learned later that they liked the movie and the movie's star, Gregory Peck, so much that his name, Gregory, ended up on my birth certificate. This was fortunate. The name "Atticus" would have been a lot to live up to.

To Kill a Mockingbird later became one of my favorite books. Much later, when my wife Kelly was expecting, we considered the name "Scout" if our baby was to be a girl. And while Scout would've been a cute name, I don't think Harper Lee gave it to the protagonist of her novel because she thought it was cute. As Lee deals with themes of racial injustice, courage, compassion, and, perhaps most of all, seeing things rightly, she is telegraphing to us something important with her main character's compelling name.

Jean Louise Finch, the scrappy young heroine we come to know as Scout, ventures into the terrain of the Deep South in the 1930s, reporting back to us as our narrator with an innocent but unvarnished eye. Because as a child she cannot fully fathom the scope and magnitude of the prejudice and hate before her, its wickedness is revealed to us all the more powerfully. She's telling us what's out there. She has an uncomplicated relationship with the truth. She's a scout.

Julia Galef is the founder of the Center for Applied Rationality. While her work has nothing to do with *To Kill a Mockingbird*, Galef promotes the same idea that Harper Lee's novel does: to see rightly what is immediately before us. Galef presents us with a stark choice: *Do we want to navigate our way through life with the mindset of a soldier or that of a scout?*

A literal scout's job, Galef tells us, is not to attack or to defend.[1] A scout's job is to look and listen to what's before her—to understand, to map out the terrain, to identify the obstacles encountered, to keep asking questions, and to find the way through. It's a scout's job not to fight but *to know what's out there* so that she may traverse the unknown safely, see things accurately and with precision, and then report back to help others across.

While sometimes a soldier's mindset is necessary, such a mindset often leads to becoming constrained into win/lose binaries and zero-sum games. It tends to construct its own narrative of the lay of the land, bending the facts on the ground to conform to its prior beliefs. A scout instead continually cross-examines her prior assumptions. The scout is not only open to being wrong but is also intrigued with the notion of changing her mind if that's what the topography calls for.

The ground has shifted now beneath our feet. We're in new territory, and, perhaps more than ever, we're being summoned to take up the mindset of a scout, not a soldier. We stand astride some terrible, convulsive events: the COVID-19 pandemic, the killing of George Floyd, an economic crisis, an attack on our Capitol, and so much more. Sometimes when terrible things happen, our instinct is to fall into a soldier's mindset, but that doesn't seem like what the topography is telling us to do right now.

What if, just as a scout in the wilderness would do, we try to stop and listen to what's all around us right now, especially the voices and sounds we've tended to close ourselves off from? What if we begin considering it a virtue, not a failure or a liability, to change our minds when faced with ample evidence of new terrain? What if God is asking us right now to open up our eyes a little wider, to hold things not more tightly but more loosely, and not with fear but with the mindset and the bearing of a scout?

> God, help me to find a stance toward the world that is more agile, more flexible, and more graceful right now. May my eyes be open to the path of suffering others have tread, as well as the rocks and rills of the present terrain. Let me adopt the mindset of a scout, guided by your hand, true and righteous. Uncomplicate my relationship with the truth. Where I've strained the passions of my brothers and my sisters, may I humbly pay the debt demanded by the aspiration of true equality. May I loosen my grip both on what I think I know and on power itself in order to secure the bonds of affection that remain. And as I traverse the shifting ground, as I go over, help me to see things rightly. Amen.

CHAPTER 47

TARES

The world seems inordinately messy right now, which has directed my attention to what is known as the Parable of the Tares. In it, Jesus likens the kingdom of heaven to a man who sows good seed in his field. However, while the man is sleeping, his enemy comes to sow tares—that is, weeds—over and in the midst of the wheat, and then he goes away. When the crop begins to grow, the man's servants ask him if they should pull up the weeds. He responds like this:

> No, lest when you're gathering the tares, you uproot, at the same time with it, the wheat. Permit both to grow together until the harvest, and in the strategic season of the harvest, I'll say to the harvesters, "Gather first the tares and bind them in bundles for the purpose of burning, but the wheat gather together into my granary, into my barn." (Matt 13:29-30, Kenneth Wuest's Expanded Greek Translation)

If this means what it seems to say, then maybe God's sovereign rule over the world isn't as straightforward as we might imagine. Jesus is telling us that the roots of the bad tares and good wheat are so intertwined that you can't weed out the tares without tearing out the wheat. He seems to be saying that God sees all the terrible things in the world, all the evil acts we humans do to one another, and God's response to it is this: *Good and evil. Let them grow together.*

But why?

It's an obvious question to which we have no acceptable answer except to take seriously what the parable tells us—that in the theatre of human-kind, good and evil are as inextricable in the world as they are in our own hearts, and once sown, they can't be separated. But this is especially hard to absorb in a season when it seems like the tares are not only present but present in droves. Sometimes it appears that the tares have taken over the whole field and are choking it to death. It seems that when such permission or allowance for evil is granted, the world becomes a field of tares.

At 9:42 on September 11, 2001, in light of the attacks in New York and Washington DC, Ben Sliney, chief of air-traffic-control operations at the FAA's command center in Herndon, Virginia, *on his first day on the job*, gave the unprecedented order to ground over 4,000 planes across the nation and redirect any in the sky to the nearest airport.[1] Canadian authorities began receiving diverted flights but were justifiably reluctant to take American flights into Canada's major cities, so they looked for remote airports large enough to accommodate big commercial aircraft. The city of Gander in Newfoundland had a population of only 10,000 and had an international airport, as it had previously served as a refueling stop for transatlantic flights. Gander immediately opened up its runways to receive thirty-eight airplanes that morning.

The city lacked the infrastructure to take in the nearly 8,000 passengers who were stranded, passengers from more than a hundred countries, but they filled their schools, community rooms, and churches with cots for the next three days. Bakeries and restaurants stayed open twenty-four hours a day. Hospitals staffed up while many in the town opened their homes to the "plane people," as they were called, cooking them fancy meals befitting guests, even letting them borrow their cars and caring for their pets.

No one in Gander would accept money for what they were doing. So when stranded passenger Shirley Brooks-Jones, a fundraiser at Ohio State University, reboarded her flight after three days in Gander, she asked each of her fellow passengers to contribute to a scholarship fund she was starting for the town's children. When they landed in Atlanta, Georgia, she had already raised over $15,000. The fund has now grown to $2 million and scholarships have been received by 228 students from the Gander area. Canadian's then Prime Minister, Jean Chrétien, summed up what had occurred: "9/11," he said, "will live long in memory as a day of terror and grief, but thanks to countless acts of kindness and compassion done for those stranded visitors, it will live also in memory as a day of comfort and of healing."[2]

Three days after the attacks of September 11, Diane Cardwell, Glenn Collins, Winnie Hue, Andrew Jacobs, Lynda Richardson, Joyce Wadler, and Janny Scott, six reporters from the *New York Times*, divided a stack of missing-person flyers collected from lower Manhattan and began dialing the phone numbers on the flyers and speaking to family members. Then they began to write not obituaries but stories, anecdotes, telling details that revealed the truthful good of the invariably remarkable souls who perished on 9/11. As you read these short essays, typically just a couple hundred words about each life lost, you begin to absorb, in the place where you are most human, the sublime beauty of our everyday existence and of the extraordinary that resides within the ordinary. You are struck by the unforced dedication that animated not only those who perished but also the countless millions who quietly go about their lives as wives, husbands, life partners, parents, students, employers, employees, traders, teachers, coaches, clerks, window washers, investment bankers, security guards, police chiefs, and pastry chefs, all who love to sing and draw and dance, who humbly and kindly go about their lives doing the little things each day on which true religion and faith in God and in humanity is based.[3]

After reading even a few dozen of the almost three thousand essays, you become completely and immutably persuaded that *we live in a wheat field, not a field of tares.* For while there is a tragic mystery in the presence and persistence of evil, human beings also have an undeniable capacity for kindness and selflessness that emerges reliably and durably, like wheat among the tares, under the duress that evil brings.

There's a poem by a Polish writer, a devout Catholic named Adam Zagajewski who taught creative writing at the University of Houston. In these excerpts from his stirring poem, he evokes rather than describes how wheat and tares *grow* alongside one another, tells how hope persists and returns in the wake of devastation, and, perhaps most crucially, suggests what our stance ought to be toward the God who, having created the field and the wheat itself, mourns its tares with us.

The poem is titled "Try to Praise the Mutilated World":

Try to praise the mutilated world.
. . . .
You've seen the refugees going nowhere,
You've heard the executioners sing joyfully.
You should praise the mutilated world.
. . . .
You gathered acorns in the park in autumn
and leaves eddied over the earth's scars.
Praise the mutilated world
and the gray feather a thrush lost,
and the gentle light that strays and vanishes
and returns.[4]

God, may my life be like the wheat that grows with the tares. I pray that, like poetry, the faith you give to me has the power to become a part of restoring the mutilated world. Amen.

CHAPTER 48

FORGIVENESS

But remember this, my brother
See in this some higher plan
You must use this precious silver
To become an honest man.

By the witness of the martyrs
By the Passion and the Blood
God has raised you out of darkness
I have bought your soul for God!
—The Bishop of Digne, *Les Misérables (The Musical)*

Les Misérables is one of my favorite musicals. It may be one of yours. While I've seen the musical twice and watched the most recent film version of the story a couple of times, I've started but never finished Victor Hugo's epic novel on which the musical and movie are based. The reason for my failure to finish reading this and so many other classic novels is that these literary giants like Tolstoy, Dickens, Eliot, and Dostoevsky spend so much time setting out the lengthy histories of their minor characters.

So it is with Hugo. The first dense fifty to seventy-five pages of his epic thousand-page novel deal not with any of the main characters but with a minor one, the Bishop of Digne. The long description of his life and times then leads up to the moment the book's action begins as the story's main protagonist, paroled convict Jean Valjean, arrives at the bishop's church asking for a place to stay the night. The bishop graciously accepts him, feeds him, and gives him a place to sleep. In response, Valjean steals the church's silver cutlery and flees. The police capture Valjean and take him back to the church, but even before the police inform the bishop they've found the church's silver in Valjean's knapsack, the bishop, recognizing what has occurred, speaks up, telling the police that he'd *given* the silver to Valjean as a gift. This, and what happens next, is the hinge moment, the turning point in Valjean's life, and he sets out on a different path. From here, the story we think of as *Les Misérables* is set in motion.

What one does not experience in either the stage musical or the movie is that this was not a single moment of grace and heroism on the part of the Bishop of Digne. Before this episode occurs with Valjean, we have spent some five dozen pages learning who the bishop is, his character, his motivation. We learn that, despite holding this high office, this good man is all the while acting like a common, compassionate country priest. The bishop has moved into a small, clinic-like hospital building so that the huge episcopal palace he is supposed to live in, given his title, can be used as the actual hospital for the town. He keeps only a tenth of his salary, giving the rest to the poor. He is described this way: "There are men who work hard, digging for gold; he worked hard, digging for pity. The misery of the world was his mine. Pain everywhere was an occasion for goodness always. *Love one another:* He declared this to be complete, desired nothing more; it was the sum total of his doctrine."[1]

An earlier section of the book explains his methods:

> On his rounds, he was giving and gentle and he didn't preach so much as chat. He never represented a virtue as though it were beyond an ordinary person's reach. He never drummed up far-fetched arguments or examples. . . .
>
> If he lacked examples, he made up parables that went straight to the point, with few pretty phrases and lots of images—with the same eloquence as Jesus Christ himself, sincere and persuasive. . . .
>
> He was never quick to condemn and he always took into account the surrounding circumstances. He would say, "Let's see how this sin came to pass." . . .
>
> He knew exactly how to sit and keep quiet for hours at a stretch by the side of a man who had lost the woman he loved, the mother who had lost her child. Just as he knew when to keep quiet, he also knew when to say something. . . . He did not seek to efface pain in forgetfulness, he sought to elevate it and to dignify it with hope. . . .
>
> He visited the poor whenever he had money, and when he had none, he visited the rich . . . .[2]

Hugo concludes his description of the bishop like this: "As you can see, he had a strange idiosyncratic way of looking at things. *I suspect he got it from the Gospel.*"[3]

When the police bring Jean Valjean back to the Bishop with a pack full of the church's stolen silver, the Bishop, with the police officers present, asks Valjean, "Why didn't you take the candlesticks with the rest? My dear friend, before you go, here they are. Take them. Now, go in peace."

It's certainly one of the most moving and unforgettable scenes in all of literature—a stirring act of beauty and mercy and a picture of the face of God. But what you would miss unless you read the book is that this is not an extraordinary action by the bishop; it is something fully in keeping with his character. Such an act, such behavior, was integral to his personality. It was simply the way he lived.

Forgiveness seems so hard *because it is*. We are human, and forgiveness is a divine act, but Hugo's lengthy rendition of the bishop's long and steady life of devotion to the spirit of the gospel and the example of Christ is a lesson for us. Forgiveness doesn't typically emerge from nowhere, and extraordinary grace and mercy in human beings doesn't just spring suddenly from the ether. It must be cultivated.

If you're fed up, at your wit's end, and having a hard time forgiving someone in this challenging time, just read the first fifty pages of Hugo's *Les Misérables*. Grace. This is where it comes from. This is how to cultivate it and nurture it. It flows from goodness over time and is not perhaps as mysterious as we think.

> God, help me to see the long game and to play the long game. Help me to not get caught up in the moment, reacting to being wronged, but to decide in my heart long before being *in* such a moment that I will be a person of grace, one who knows what is most important. If I am committed to bringing heaven to earth, I must transport things like grace, mercy, and forgiveness. May I do this such that, at least to some small degree, your face is reflected in mine. Amen.

CHAPTER 49

A BUMP OF
WELL-BEING

I don't typically chat up taxi drivers. It's not my thing. Being an introvert, I typically settle into the backseat and keep to myself the way God intended. These drivers have a job to do. I let them do it. However, a while back I was in London with my family, and the "All London" cab drivers in their boxy black cabs are an irrepressible lot. When our driver greeted us, I asked him about his job, which, it turned out, was like rolling the ball out onto the court for the Globetrotters. He entertained us the rest of our trip through the city.

He fascinated us with something called, "The Knowledge."[1] The Knowledge is the series of tests you have to pass to receive the "green badge" that entitles you to drive one of these London cabs. It's said to be the hardest test of any kind in the world. Each candidate must memorize over 25,000 streets, tens of thousands of landmarks, and the fastest, most direct routes between *all of them*. Tourist destinations, historic spots, museums, parks, churches, theaters. *Everything*. As they study, the candidates' minds become living, breathing navigation systems. Neuroscientists have even discovered that the posterior hippocampus, the area of the brain most crucial for memory, grows as those in the program progress through the process. Their brains acquire a sort of superpower as they prepare for their tests by riding around the city on a bike or rented moped, studying shortcuts and little-known passages, experiencing traffic patterns, reading and memorizing maps, and honing geographic intuitions that don't show up on maps. The overall process takes two to four years to finish, with many candidates dropping out or failing along the way due to the demanding time commitment, the psychological pressures, or the sheer difficulty as high-stress written tests and unforgiving oral exams are administered before one is allowed to receive the privilege of operating a taxi around the London metropolitan area completely by memory.

Exiting the cab, I felt the happiness of connection, of having been deeply enriched by another human being. Yet, even after this scintillating experience, for some reason I still often feel a resistance to speaking to people in these situations. For me at least, there's typically a start-up cost paid in the clumsy currency of social awkwardness when I try to connect like this to neighbors, to people I'm standing with in line, to baristas, to Uber drivers, and to others—even to folks I sort of know.

Nick Epley is a professor of Behavioral Science at the University of Chicago. He studies things like this, and his research impressively suggests that these little dialogues, even the fleeting conversation fragments we have in public spaces with each other, reliably notch up our mood. The little effort expended to show genuine interest in another person—even a friendly wave on the street or the positive exchange of smiles—gives us a measurable bump of well-being. Conversely, the absence of these connections in our day reliably decreases our mood, diminishes our general affect, and reduces our sense of well-being. Epley insists that we vastly underestimate how much we're affected when we reach out to each other in a positive ways.[2]

All this to say that, if you're like me, you may be systematically failing to do something that will not only make you happier but that is what Christ, a curious combination of introvert/extrovert himself, calls us to do—to be a presence for good in the lives of our neighbors, to offer friendship, and to connect to those in need, knowing that much of the time these needs remain invisible until such an exchange occurs.

So take some baby steps or next steps, connecting with folks you don't know just a bit more. If it goes better than you think, be mindful of how it makes you feel. Or if you're good at it already, maybe turn up your empathy dials, calibrating your listening skills even more. Find your voice. Fine tune your ears. You might even find that you have a new superpower.

> God, help me break down the barriers between what I think of as my religious life and what I think of as my actual life so that I can simply be an active presence for good in the lives of my neighbors and the strangers I encounter, offering moments of friendship and solidarity, connecting to those in need, knowing needs are often invisible until I do. Help me to strike up meaningful conversations. Surprise me. Help me to feel the bump of well-being on offer to me during this time, especially, as I find my authentic voice in public spaces in this bustling world, for your kingdom. Amen.

CHAPTER 50

PILOT

When I was a kid, I loved Houston's marvelous and eclectic local amusement park called AstroWorld. My favorite attraction was The River of No Return, a riverboat ride that entailed floating along and through a series of scenes from exotic locales around the world. As the ride began and the boat pulled away from the dock, the captain would always ask a kid to come up and take the wheel. I had an uncanny knack for getting this job. It was probably the distinct air of leadership and competence I exuded as a seven-year-old. Or maybe it was that my dad told them it was my birthday. Regardless, I'd step forward with a look of deep concentration, knowing all the passengers were now depending solely on me to navigate them through the river's many twists and turns, avoiding the waterfalls, rocks, dangerous rapids, and rudimentary audio-animatronic wildlife found along the way.

Imagine my disappointment later when I learned that the vessel remained under control of the real captain all along. The corporate heads and legal department representing AstroWorld surely knew it was ill-advised to let a child like me drive a boat. Not only did I lack the requisite experience to operate a pleasure craft full of passengers, but my prefrontal cortex wasn't close to being developed enough to make all the right choices to get us back to the dock and safely home.

The prefrontal cortex is what allows captains, pilots, and drivers—all of us—to plan ahead, to predict the consequences of our own actions, and to anticipate the actions of others. It's what gives us the ability to put ourselves in someone else's skin. It's what allows us to run a series of *pilot-like* simulations, to play things out, in our imaginations before acting and moving forward. It's what gives us the capability to perform thought experiments and then decide on the best course ahead.

David French is a conservative writer, a veteran, and a religious man. He and his wife have three kids: a blonde-haired son, a blue-eyed daughter, and a beautiful Ethiopian daughter, Naomi, whom they adopted. He has written about how Naomi's experience has differed vastly from that of his other kids. People see Naomi at the community swimming pool and ask where her parents are. She's been followed in department stores. Some of the incidents could have benign explanations, but as they multiplied, the benign explanations became increasingly implausible. French's recent writing encourages us to use our prefrontal cortex as God intends and run a thought experiment like this:

Suppose one in ten White Americans is racist. Perhaps that's off. Maybe that's generous. It's hard to say, but let's keep going. Consider that in many places, racism is not only condemned but is stigmatized such that those who do hold such views remain silent to maintain their social standing. If you're White and live in such a place, you're unlikely to hear racist remarks much, if at all.[1]

Now imagine you're Black or brown, and 10 percent of the White people you encounter think less of you, are suspicious of you, or even hate you because of your skin color. "You don't know in advance who they are or how they'll react to you," French writes, "but they'll be present enough to be at best a persistent source of pain and at worst a source of actual danger." You'll be pulled over more. Store clerks will follow you. Many of your encounters will be strangely hostile. You're reasonably told to live on guard. Risk could arise at any time. It's simply part of the fabric of your life. "This," French writes, "is how we live in a world where a white person can say of racism, 'Where is it?' and a black person can say, 'How can you not see?' It's how one set of Americans can say, 'It's so much better than it was,' and another say, 'You're still not listening.'"

Psalm 139 says we are "fearfully and wonderfully made." We are. *We're pilots.* Every day, we run hundreds of thought experiments. Some, it turns out, are of deep spiritual consequence. God has given us the remarkable ability to simulate one another's experience. To run this particular simulation is a gospel function. When Christ said, "do unto others as you would have them do unto you," he was asking us to do precisely this. To be a pilot. It's the only way home.

> God, help me to replicate within my imagination the lived experience of others. I acknowledge that I should have done this better long ago. May I sense the rough currents fought, the turbulence, and the shear. May I see what is required to ford the river each day. May I feel the historic obstacles crashed against and all that must be resiliently endured even now simply to go out, to live, to provide, and to get back home again. May I run this simulation until I see it so clearly that it directs my future ways and shows me who I must become. Amen.

CHAPTER 51

RESOLUTE. INTREPID. ONWARD.

The United States Navy is skilled at many things, and not least among these is how it names its vessels. There are ships called the *Audacious*, the *Brave*, the *Comfort*, the *Defiance*, the *Dauntless*, the *Hope*, the *Sturdy*, the *Tranquility*, and the *Victorious*, but my favorites are the *Resolute*, the *Intrepid*, and the *Onward*.

As we continue to press ahead through a season of "semi staying put," its precipitant medical storm, and all the accompanying economic headwinds, I hope that these three words provide heightened courage to face what's still before you, displacing any sense of fear or anxiety present or just ahead in your life.

Resolute. Intrepid. Onward.

As you offer your prayer to God, breathe these words in and out. Let them elevate your spirit, renew your mind, and fill the gaps between your heart's uncertainties. Keep them close to inspire and lift your soul above the choppy waterline as you forge ahead, caring for yourself and for others.

> God, direct me toward the sustenance I need and to all that strengthens me—to sunlight, to good conversation, to movement, to meaningful work, and to rest. Grant me resilience. Restore me from exhaustion. I resolve to brighten your world with Christ's light. I shall try never to cause your creation to be dimmed. I am resolute.
>
> *Resolute. Intrepid. Onward.*
>
> God, though physically restricted, let me be an explorer, pursuing through mind and heart a new intimacy with you, a new closeness with those I love, and new currents that lead me toward new places in which I may serve. In these pursuits, I pray for adventure. I am intrepid.
>
> *Resolute. Intrepid. Onward.*
>
> God, help me to shed old ways that have outlasted their usefulness. Unshackle me from sin and waste.

Calm my fears and tendency to worry. Steady me. Help me to forgive, to forbear, and to pioneer in the ways of mercy. Rudder my life more closely to that of Christ's. I pray for forward progress. Onward.

Resolute. Intrepid. Onward.

Finally, God, I seek your healing for those in need all around me. Bestow endurance to the beleaguered, safe harbor for those serving in the storm, buoyant hope to those adrift in sorrow and in pain, and for all, O God, a hastening toward blue skies ahead.

Resolute. Intrepid. Onward.

Amen.

CHAPTER 52

A LONGER RUNWAY

A few years ago, I took on the role of commissioner of our neighborhood's fall baseball little league. One of the responsibilities of the job was to recruit managers for all the teams. One dad whom I didn't know contacted me about wanting to coach a team. He seemed knowledgeable and nice and passed all the background checks, so he became the manager of his son's team, the nine-year-old Mets. However, when the season began, we received complaints from two moms whose kids were on this team because the manager was leading the team in a Christian prayer before the games. I called the two mothers who had spoken out. Both were reasonable and polite. Their families were of non-Christian faith traditions and said the prayers made both of them and both of their nine-year-old sons confused and uncomfortable given the context of a little league game.

I next called the manager, explained the situation, and told him he was, of course, welcome to pray with his own child, but I respectfully asked him to refrain from praying with the whole team. To my surprise, he said no. He told me this was a matter of principle for him and he had no plans to stop. He said to stop praying would not be a good message to his son. I then told him that, as a minister, I was sensitive to his convictions, but if he persisted with the team or excluded those of other faiths, we'd have to make a change. This predictably made him upset, and he lamented the state of the country, the state of the league, the state of baseball, and my leadership in general, and said he wouldn't quit. I tried to negotiate a little more, but when he wouldn't budge, I told him I was sorry, but I'd have to ask him to step down, which I did, and we had to get the Mets a new manager.

The situation left me wondering whether this manager was being the kind of bold witness of Christ that God wants in the world or, given the circumstances, doing something wrong, as I sensed he was. I am still open to the possibility that I was wrong and he was right or that some other principled compromise would have been a better course.

Ron Chernow, in his recent biography of Ulysses Grant, writes that General Grant had a distinct genius, an instinct, for seeing and understanding topography.[1] He had a mathematical grasp of the terrain he found himself on, whatever its nature. He intuitively comprehended the contours and the altitudes, the advantages and the disadvantages of the ground on which a battle was to be waged, thus providing him a real edge over his opposition.

When it comes to how people look at faith and Christianity in particular, you may instinctively sense or know the cultural terrain we're on as believers, but let me lay it out a bit more in order to then address how we might better talk about our faith to our neighbors. From 2004 to 2007, the Barna Research Group conducted a series of surveys.[2] They gave thousands of men and women ages sixteen to twenty-nine (who must by now be in their late twenties, thirties, and forties) some words and asked them if the words described present-day Christianity. Here's what they found:

The first word was *judgmental*, and 87 percent of those asked said, yes, I think of present-day (2004–2007) Christians as judgmental. The next word was *hypocritical*, and 85 percent said yes, it's been my experience that Christians are hypocritical. And it went on from there: *too political*, 75 percent; *anti-gay*, 91 percent; *not accepting of other faiths*, 64 percent. This is not advantageous ground, and my guess is that it's gotten worse, not better, since the survey was conducted. So what do we do against these difficult cultural headwinds and unappealing ground?

We humans are wired to be influenced, especially in matters of the heart, mainly through ongoing one-on-one relationships with people we trust and have come to respect. A few years ago, I attended a fundraiser for a charity that provides mentors and fellowship for kids with parents in the military, and one of my oldest friends, Brad Kearney, was the speaker for the event. Brad and I taught a Bible study to middle schoolers together when we were both in high school. While I'm still not sure who thought that was a good idea, I at least became good friends with Brad in the process. After high school, Brad attended and graduated from the Air Force Academy, became an officer, flew combat missions, and, later in his career, commanded a squadron. Brad is one of those guys who does things with excellence everywhere he goes but still manages to stay affable and approachable.

Brad said that while he served as the commanding officer for a squadron, people of all sorts, of all faiths or lack of faith, under his command would come to him for advice, especially when crises arose. He would give them practical counsel based on his many years of professional experience. He wears his wisdom lightly, but I expect those who came to see him recognized it. Most of the time, he said, he would just do a lot of listening, but at the end he'd try to point them toward a practical plan of action. Following this, Brad would then add a question. He'd ask the person before him if they were interested in hearing some additional faith-based suggestions that had always helped him when he was in a difficult spot. And if they responded positively, then, changing neither the tone of his voice nor the character of the room, Brad would sensitively—and in a way tailored to the situation and person—speak about God's love and his own faith in Christ. He would explain that this is what he had leaned on throughout his life and career.

Brad had *earned* an opportunity to speak frankly and honestly by demonstrating a genuine interest in the life of the person who was seeking help at their own point of need. This sort of approach requires, as Brad himself might say, more runway. It requires a kind and graceful listening ear, a willingness to lift or share burdens like loneliness or uncertainty, a readiness to provide timely assistance with kids or aging parents, and the patience and understanding to walk through things like broken relationships, addictions, and legal or medical problems. You have to *earn* opportunities to speak about crucial matters of faith like this. It might require patience and finesse that is born more from love and human compassion than evangelical fervor. The thing is, though, especially in these troubled days, the opportunities are everywhere if we're willing to patiently taxi a bit along the runway.

> God, may I be open-hearted, especially now, to speak of Christ to others. Help me to build more runway, to earn the opportunities to share the sacred not so much *to* as *with* those I encounter at their point of need. Amen.

CHAPTER 53

SECOND MILE

I was once hired to defend a woman who had been brought into an unusual lawsuit. She was a clerk at a dry-cleaning and shoe-repair business. The woman who had sued her was a customer who used the drive-thru window to pick up her dry-cleaning. The clerk had retrieved her clothes, rung up the sale, told the customer how much it was, and made the exchange—but then everything went sideways. Instead of driving away, the customer looked at the receipt and became convinced that she'd been overcharged. So she waved, and the clerk returned to the window and reviewed the charges one by one with her, explaining their accuracy. The customer was still unconvinced and demanded to see the manager. The clerk responded that she was the only employee there, but she provided a card with the manager's name and number on it as she was trained to do. This still wasn't good enough for the customer, and she announced that she wasn't leaving until she received the disputed amount back, which was something like a dollar and eighty-seven cents. The line was backing up behind her and my client, the clerk, refused to give back the money, which further enraged the customer.

The situation quickly escalated. The two hurled insults at each other until the customer fully lost her temper and began to try to reach up from her car to strike the clerk through the window. Under assault, the clerk grabbed the nearest thing she could find—a recently repaired high-heeled shoe—and subdued the irate customer with an unfortunate but well-struck blow to her eye with the business end of the high-heeled shoe.

The case went to trial, and as we were picking the jury, one of the potential jurors spoke up with the question that was surely foremost on everyone's mind. "So," he asked, "am I right that this whole deal is really over a dollar and eighty-seven cents?"

His implication was spot on. Some fights should never happen and aren't worth having. There's something to be said for knowing when to walk away from a fight. This is an important skill to develop, but what about engaging with others—family, neighbors, friends—in matters of public controversy, the sort of disputes that often lead to fights, contempt, grudges, and fractured relationships? Especially in these edgy days of social upheaval, political rivalry, ongoing fatigue, deep uncertainty, low trust, and high anxiety, *what are the rules of engagement?*

We could start by remembering this idea embedded in the middle of the Sermon on the Mount: *If anyone forces you to go one mile, go with them two miles* (Matt 5:41).

Most of us probably learned this verse as an exhortation to go farther physically and further spiritually than the average person in being kind, forbearing, and graceful. So, taking this as our jumping off point, what might going the second mile look like as we interact on matters of public controversy in such a highly polarized, acutely stressed season of life?

Here are six second-mile, non-contempt-generating suggestions for us to consider taking up at this moment:

First, *defend someone with whom you disagree who is being bullied or abused by your allies*, the people on your side of an argument. Second, *stop picking nuts*. Nut-picking is the style of argument that points to something extreme that someone on your opponent's side said or did and then portrays that offensive thing as emblematic of the entirety of your opponent's thinking. Stop doing this—that is, stop punching down. Third, we must *confess our own sins, not those of others*. Fourth, if we're shooting for civility and tolerance in our encounters, we're aiming too low and ought to recalibrate to something much more subversive. *Re-aim for love.* Focus on your opponent's distress, not to exploit it but to tend it. Then listen to understand and not to rebut. Fifth, when you feel that contempt bubbling up, rising up in your heart in response to something someone has said or done, remember, there's probably a child or little old lady down the street with an unmet need. *Consider diverting your energy and attention to someone in need.* And finally, sixth, *recall that not every bad thing in the world requires a response.* If you're about to become embroiled in a disagreement over something akin to a dry-cleaning bill, recognize it—call it a dollar and eighty-seven cent dry-cleaning bill, and take a deep breath. Put the shoe down, and step away from the window.

> God, may I be someone who stands up for others but isn't quite so fast to stand up when it's me who is offended. May I be someone who is committed to taking the temperature down. Help me, on matters of controversy, to open hearts and not close them. Help me not to generate contempt but to nurture grace at each mile marker ahead. Amen.

CHAPTER 54

WEAVING OUR WAY HOME

We were in Galveston. I was eight. My brother David was nine and my sisters were younger. Our family was on a long weekend summer trip. We were staying at Gaido's Seaside Inn, the one on Seawall Boulevard next to the Gaido's Restaurant that used to have a giant crab on top of the roof. For a kid, spending all day in the ocean, eating fried shrimp at night, and falling asleep to the sound of the waves along the Gulf of Mexico was as good as it gets.

On the final day of the trip, David, my dad, and I went down the seawall toward Stewart Beach where they had set up a cheap little traveling carnival. It smelled of fish, the staff was surly, and intuitively I sensed that the attractions were unsafe, most notably the fun house that, if I recall, was named "The Dark Maze of Doom" or something like that. Dad stayed outside, but David and I went in and found ourselves in a long, dark hallway, which soon led to another dark hallway, and then another. What was it like? You know how it is when you go into a dark theater; you have to wait a little, but soon enough your eyes get adjusted. Well, it was like that, only in The Dark Maze of Doom your eyes never adjust. It's just dark. And it stays dark. David and I forged ahead, but then somehow we got separated.

Alone now, I recall wondering how, given the nature and dilapidated condition of the whole carnival operation, its owners had mastered the science behind eliminating every conceivable photon of light in this forsaken place. I was absolutely lost in pure, metaphysical darkness. Even though light, safety, and my dad were just a few feet away outside the walls of the awful maze, there was no way I could get to him. Finally, between my sobs and after what seemed like an eternity, I heard, some distance away, David's voice calling my name, and in hearing his voice I gathered the courage to call back. I was alone no longer. He found me. Together now, we sensed some light a few turns ahead and slowly wove our way out and eventually home. And though I wouldn't (and couldn't) articulate it this way until much later, I learned a gospel lesson that day: that even when light, security, and your own Father is near, when you're lost, alone, and in the dark, it sometimes takes your brother to rescue you.

We now have reams and reams of research showing that, although we are a richer society, more knowledgeable about the world, and in some ways more connected to each other than ever before, many of us feel unhappier, more isolated, and less fulfilled than ever before. And if we ask why that is, the conclusion of most social scientists who study this sort of thing is that our communities simply aren't as cohesive and our institutions aren't as strong as they once were. Harvard professor Robert Putnam calls this phenomenon an evaporation of social capital.[1] Over the last several decades, he says, the relationships, connections, and institutions that have long helped us navigate the world have dried up. For instance, a quarter of Americans say they have no close friends at all—no one in whom to confide about important matters, no one with whom to share life's joys and burdens. A full third of those over forty-five years of age confess that chronic loneliness is a fundamental challenge for them. We are, as many have said, in the middle of a loneliness epidemic.

In the Old Testament book of Ecclesiastes, a book in which God is not mentioned much at all, we find this:

> Two are better than one because they have a good return for their labor. If either of them falls down, one can help the other up. But pity anyone who falls and has no one to help them up. Also, if two lie down together, they will keep each other warm. But how can one keep warm alone? And though one may be overpowered, two can defend themselves, and a cord of three strands is not quickly broken. (Eccl 4:9-12)

Quite straightforwardly, this writer, whom some call the *Quester*, tells us that it's only with friends, among community, and in relationship that we survive and flourish as human beings. It's in communion with one another that we find the elusive meaning we look for but fail to find in so many other places. In short, the Quester tells us that it takes a sibling to keep us from becoming hopelessly lost in the great maze of darkness our world sometime presents.

It's easy somehow to overlook that God is present to us *in one another.* Both Ecclesiastes and modern social scientists seem to be telling us with great confidence that we weave social fabric and a sense of flourishing back into our lives by working toward a "yes" on these four questions:

1. Do you have a family you love and who love you?
2. Do you have friends you trust and can confide in?
3. Do you have work that matters to you?
4. Do you have a worldview that can make sense of suffering and death?

How do you answer the big four? I'm struck by how a "yes" to all of these questions is offered to us each week, even in our speedy modern world, in something known as *the local church*. Maybe you feel lost in the dark in the maze of this present moment. If you're looking for a remarkably efficient *meaning-generating engine* to begin to propel you out of the darkness, even if you're not particularly sure about the depth of your faith or if you have one at all, the church, despite its faults as a human institution, might be a good place to start.

My friend Earlene Rentz Turner is a gifted composer. She was commissioned to write a piece about what's on offer to us through the church when we are lost in darkness. It's surprising that there are not a lot songs in the hymnal about an elemental truth of our faith—that Christ, in this sometimes dizzying current age, incarnates miraculously like light among us as the local church beckoning us home. I was asked to help write the lyrics, and in what became an edifying collaboration, these words emerged:

My soul the dark of night beheld,
And searched in vain for trouble's ease,
When far away a church bell pealed,
"Come find God's blessing and God's peace."

For here a light, a miracle
Is Christ and kindred company,
All welcome here as family,
To find God's blessing and God's peace.

In love and care, we bind our hearts,
In friendship's peace is pain's release,
In unison, we raise one voice
To sing God's blessing and God's peace.

As God now holds you in our arms,
Arise, assured you are not alone.
Your voice, the toll of grace shall be,
To share God's blessing and God's peace.

For here a light, a miracle
Is Christ and kindred company,
All welcome here as family,
To share God's blessing and God's peace.

God, when I feel lost in the dark, may I remember
that, in addition to having you nearby, I can also rely
on those with whom I worship for love and friendship,
for guidance, and for comfort in times of uncertainty.
Help me both to find and to renew these connections
in order to weave my way out and eventually home.
Amen.

CHAPTER 55

TAKING THE "L"

In the midst of a strange sports season, when we've had baseball, basketball, football, and hockey all going on at once, I'm reminded of a comment my friend Rod Richardson made as we were discussing St. Paul's take on suffering. Rod said, "I guess it's true that we learn from suffering, but as human beings we still hate to take the 'L.'" Well-crafted athletic metaphors typically ring true to me, and this one did because, like most of us, I hate losing. There are a few little league losses my boys sustained years ago that still sting when I think about them—which I still do with laughable regularity.

There's a great line in the baseball movie *Moneyball* in which the Oakland A's general manager Billy Beane, following a devastating defeat in the American League playoffs, responds to a colleague's suggestion that he'll get over the loss. "I never get over these things," he responds, and he's not alone. Why is that? Why is losing so corrosive, and why does its sting last? Maybe it's because losing delivers us a unique kind of psychological blow.

Here's my theory: we're told and believe not only that the world operates according to certain rules but also that we naturally see ourselves as the heroic figure in the narrative of our own lives. Everything we experience, as the late writer David Foster Wallace put it, we see and take in from our own point of view, as the center of our little universe.[1] So when loss occurs, it doesn't seem fair. The hero is not supposed to lose; it violates the plotline. That is, we always think of *our* team as the team that *should* win, and we feel likewise that as individuals we *ought* to always prevail. And when it doesn't happen, it strikes us that things haven't turned out the way they *should.* There's a moral character to it. And in this way, every loss in a sense presents to us a mini, or sometimes not so mini, identity crisis. *What does it mean if I lose? And what does it mean if I keep losing? Who am I? What rules are operable in this world?* Our psychology doesn't seem to allow truth to leak in to convey to us that indeed, if we're human, we're going to lose sometimes, and we're liable to lose often.

With only limited success, I've begun to try to think of the experience of losing not as something I should try to shake off or get over as inconsequential but as something I should try to better integrate into my life and identity. On one hand, this might seem counterintuitive because it treats even minor losses as more existential than merited, but on the other hand, the little experiment serves a larger purpose. After all, we lose a lot, and it makes sense to think of the experience holistically. Our lives are marked by our losses. We lose our innocence. Growing up, we lose boyfriends and girlfriends. Our youthful dreams are lost. We may lose our jobs and our money. We may lose our faith. We lose family and our health. Some of us lose our memories. In some sense, life is just one loss after another until, eventually, we lose everything. We lose our lives.

Perhaps these other losses we suffer—in sports, in arguments, in political rivalry, with respect to matters at work, or even with respect to our loved ones—are all concentrically growing crises that offer us chance after chance to practice the integration of grace into our lives. That is, they're a series of sequential dress rehearsals readying us for the biggest loss of all, which we can then face with courage upon learning the ultimate power of grace.

We ought to give some serious thought about how we handle and approach loss because much of life is a question about "how we take the 'L.'" When I think of how I'll look back on this season, and on whether I've borne it well, a lot will depend on my answer to this question.

Learning to lose doesn't mean quitting, risking no more, or losing hope. It doesn't mean getting to be completely OK with losing, and it certainly doesn't mean feeling nothing or programming yourself spiritually to want nothing. But it does mean integrating adversity and loss into your life, continuing to live, and continuing to lose, but coming to know yourself better, finding grace within yourself, and then expressing that grace into a world full of brokenness and loss. This is the crucial, and maybe the only, thing that counts. It's where your humanity grows. And in it, we're liable to find not only that there's value in losing but also that losing is the most important lesson in life.

> God, I know I'm going to lose, probably a lot, and whether I benefit from these experiences is up to me. Stir up grace in me in response. Help me take the "L." Amen.

CHAPTER 56

BIG LIGHTS AND LITTLE LIGHTS

In 1995, a man named Bob Williams wanted to do an experiment. He wanted to point his telescope at a patch of sky filled with absolutely nothing for a hundred hours. It was a terrible idea and his colleagues told him so. But fortunately, Bob Williams wasn't just anybody. He was the director of STSI, the Space Telescope Science Institute, and he didn't just have any telescope; he had the Hubble Telescope.

So for a hundred hours between December 18 and December 28, 1995, the Hubble Telescope stared fixedly at a carefully chosen, small patch of absolutely nothing. And in those ten days, it took 342 pictures of, well, nothing. Or so it was thought. When the images were processed, combined, colored, and finally viewed, the pictures showed galaxies—*everywhere.* Based on Williams's seemingly quixotic experiment, the estimated number of galaxies in the universe increased from ten billion to fifty billion. Since then, similar efforts have proven that there are not just fifty billion galaxies out there but *a hundred billion—each one with hundreds of billions of stars inside them.*[1]

Every time we look up into the starry night, yes, we should surely feel a sense of the divine in the incredible distance and vastness above, but even as we do, we must not forget that the same God who created this big miracle performs *intimate miracles* inside our hearts too. The following fable is meant to remind us of what we tend to forget, that there are intimate miracles as well as big ones:

There was once a country called *Forgetful,* and in this distant place lived a people who didn't remember well. Whenever night came, they forgot that daylight would ever return. As you can probably imagine, in a nighttime full of darkness that they thought would never end, the people of Forgetful became fearful. When it was night, they began to lash out at one another, hurting one another, and doing terrible things to one another. And this got worse and worse and went on for way too long. Then, one morning, a king came and befriended the people of Forgetful. He was true, full of wonder and wisdom. He taught all of them certain rules to help when they started to forget and became scared of the dark, but what he was teaching them was not just about rules but about bright, beautiful things like love and mercy in disguise. Because they learned these lessons, these laws, a lasting peace and an enduring justice came and stayed throughout the land. However, eventually knowledge of the good king passed away, and it wasn't long until once again, the people of Forgetful forgot and at night became afraid again and hurt one another again.

Fortunately, though, after a time, the king's son came of age and befriended the people of Forgetful. He didn't just remind them about the king; he did more. Each night, he went out into the dark where people were scared, and he stayed with them all night until dawn was near. Where people were alone and in the dark, he protected them and told them it wouldn't always be this way. Where people were in despair because it was so dark, he told them never to give up. It wasn't only in what he said but also in the way he said it that gave them courage. Where people were fighting, he tried to make peace, telling them it would soon be morning and things would look different in the day. And finally, though it didn't always work, he went to those who were hurting all the others, sometimes purposely, sometimes just because they couldn't see and were scared, and he listened to what they had to say. Listening seemed to make a difference, but none of this was easy. His attempts at encouragement, peacemaking, and empathy didn't always work, and on one of these nights, when they didn't know completely what they were doing, the people pushed the king's good son off a cliff. They watched him tumble down into the dark, fall to the bottom, and die. The thing was, though, that when they turned around to go back to their houses, he appeared to them and pointed to the sky, where miraculously, a light in the darkness, a star, had now appeared. And it came to pass that the people of Forgetful began to call this star *Hope*, and when it became dark at night, because of *Hope* they no longer forgot that dawn would always come again.

The people of Forgetful didn't just leave it at that. They were inspired by the star. Where people were scared because it was dark, they stayed with them all night until dawn was near. Where people were in sorrow and in despair because it was so dark, they told them never to give up. It wasn't just what they said but also the way they said it that gave the others real courage. Where people were fighting, they tried to make peace, telling them it would soon be morning and things would look different in the day. And finally, though it didn't always work, they went to those who were hurting all the others, sometimes purposely, sometimes just because they couldn't see, and they listened to what they had to say. This seemed to make a difference somehow. It wasn't easy, but when they did this, each of them, like little lights on the ground shining like the star called *Hope* in the sky, reminded all the others that darkness is only temporary and that morning always comes even if it's hard to remember.

> God, though I live in a place so big that it reminds me I must be in awe of You, help me also to remember the miracle of love that was born in my heart because of your intimate love for me. Let this little light be a hope for others always. Amen.

CHAPTER 57

WITH THEM

The light, pure and pleasant, pours through the large windows, diffusing inside against warrens of pure white—the bright walls of what's known as the Modern Wing of the museum called the Art Institute of Chicago. It's home to hundreds of contemporary canvases painted roughly from 1900 to 1950. Many of the artists whose work graces this section of the museum fled their European homes and studios as the Nazis rose to power in the 1930s. Museum visitors speak in hushed tones, sometimes amused, sometimes awed, as bold strokes and striking color carry them along, almost dream-like, from room to room. Cezanne and Matisse, Picasso and Pisarro, Dali's surrealism, Kandinsky's abstraction. Now up on the third floor, if you weave your way through the brightness, the beauty, the different schools of art, and navigate left, then right, then left again, the painting will absolutely stop you in your tracks, arresting you not by the color that has marked the rest of the exhibit but suddenly by the lack of it. All at once, it's as if the life blood of the museum has left its body. And here you meet an artist named Marc Chagall. Russian. Jewish. Exiled.

In 1938, as Hitler declared full-fledged war against the Jews, Chagall was exiled in France, a country about to be overrun itself, and he painted the retina-burning masterpiece called *White Crucifixion*. Five feet high and almost five feet wide, it evokes a sense of tragic beauty and a lot of questions. Why is a distinctly Jewish artist painting the crucifixion of Jesus? Who are the soldiers storming in from the left? Is that a synagogue on fire to the right? Who or what are the figures floating above the cross? What's happening with the rickety boat? And who is the man in green running away with a sack on his back? *What is all this, and what does it mean?*

Art historian Simon Schama writes that the power of great art is the power to shake us.[1] It jolts us into an awakening, into revelation. It rewires us so that we apprehend the world differently.

In 1937, Hitler's minister of propaganda Joseph Goebbels confiscated the work of Marc Chagall and many other Jewish painters from German museums and put them together into a mock exhibition in Munich called *Entartete Kunst*—or Degenerate Art. In this exhibition, instead of organizing the presentation of the canvases in an orderly fashion as the Germans were obviously capable of doing, the paintings, many without frames, were chaotically nailed to the wall close together in narrow galleries or even set haphazardly on the ground. The painters and their art were derided with labels over each painting—titles like *A Mockery of German Women* and *This Is How Diseased Minds See Nature* and *Complete Madness*. To further inflame the German public in the midst of their own national depression, Goebbels saw to it that next to the artwork and the derisive labels, the prices paid for the works by the museums from which they were taken were also posted.[2]

Then, as 1937 passed into 1938, Nazi action intensified against the Jews. It became about much more than art. On June 15, 1938, hundreds of Polish Jews were loaded into trains bound for concentration camps. In August, the synagogues in Munich and Nuremberg were vandalized and then destroyed. Next, on November 9, in a coordinated attack throughout Germany, Austria, and Poland, stormtroopers ransacked Jewish homes, arresting over 100,000 Jewish men and sending them to places called Dachau and Buchenwald. Jewish cemeteries were defiled. The remainder of country's 200 synagogues were destroyed and their sacred texts burned in bonfires. In the cities, the windows of Jewish-owned storefronts and businesses were smashed, leaving shards of broken glass everywhere in what became known as *Kristallnacht*, the Night of Broken Glass. When the violence finally paused, the German Jews who had been rounded up and relocated in ghettos were fined over a billion German marks for the damage done, including four million to repair broken windows. In exile in France, Marc Chagall, his work mocked, his heritage derided, his people perse-cuted, and his life endangered, hearing reports of the terror of *Kristallnacht*, picked up his brush and in 1938 painted *White Crucifixion*.

Rather than mournful angels around Jesus on the cross, Chagall paints floating Hebrew patriarchs shielding their eyes or calling for help. The dominant color is white, which, though we associate it with purity, in Jewish heritage represents sorrow. There is a divine involvement in the angle of light that shines whiter than the rest of the whites behind the *T-shaped* cross, which is the same T-shape, called the *Tau*, that Jewish men historically wore to symbolize lamentation. On Jesus' left, as if he's reaching out for them, there's a Jewish village being stormed by soldiers. Houses tumble upside down, a fiddle lies on the ground, and a dead body lies uncovered in a desecrated Jewish graveyard. Below, near the bottom of the canvas, refugees flee by boat pitifully with only a single oar. On Jesus' right, Nazis desecrate a synagogue, its Torah ark in flames. In the bottom left-hand corner, three bearded figures, one of whom clutches the Torah, escape on foot. One man wears a German placard reading *"Ich bin Jude."* I am a Jew.

Finally, the man in the lower right-hand corner wearing green and carrying a sack is a depiction, a representation, of the wandering Jew. The legend of the wandering Jew arose in medieval times and speaks of a teacher of the law in Jesus' time, one who taunted Christ on the cross and was then, according to the myth, cursed to walk the earth until the Second Coming. Echoing the halo around a mangled menorah at his feet is the halo around Jesus' head. And within this halo of light is the inscription, *"Jesus of Nazareth, King of the Jews."* However, Chagall's Aramaic spelling is a play on words. The way he spells *Nazareth* refers not to a place, as in Jesus of Nazareth, but instead translates as *Jesus of the Nazarenes*—the Nazarenes being a common way that early Christians were denoted as being followers of Christ. Essentially, what he's written is this: *Jesus of the Christians, King of the Jews*—indicating his recognition of Jesus' importance to both Christians and Jews and tying both faiths together at this imperiled moment in 1938.

Chagall is powerfully connecting the suffering of Jesus that Christians would recognize with the vivid horrors Jews were experiencing at that moment in Europe, calling upon an international Christian audience to respond with help and with compassion, to come to save them. Chagall is telling us that the message of Christ is that there should be a unity of sorrow, that we must share in one another's suffering.

As I stood in front of the painting in Chicago, Chagall jolted me into a vision of life not so much as a long and bending narrative of rivalry and conflict between protagonists and antagonists in history but more simply as a story of God suffering with those who suffer and calling us to do the same. What Chagall, with paint and a white canvas, told me is that we are with Christ when we are with them.

> God, keep reminding me that if I want to be with You, I must be with those most in need, those who suffer. I must suffer with them. Amen.

CHAPTER 58

SOUL EXPANSION

You might not know Vinko Bogataj, but you've probably seen him. "Spanning the globe to bring you the constant variety of sport. The thrill of victory . . . *and the agony of defeat.*"

The *Wide World of Sports* was a Saturday afternoon fixture in my life growing up, a TV show I watched each week when I was a kid. The show's intro was always the same: the music and commentator Jim McKay's voice-over were iconic, but what was most memorable about the show's opening was the video of the dreadful crash of Slovenian ski jumper, Vinko Bogataj, as McKay moved from the words "the thrill of victory" to "the agony of defeat." Fortunately, Bogotaj sustained only minor injuries in the incident. Nevertheless, his misfortune was memorably cemented into the consciousness of a generation of sports fans as synonymous with the notion of terrific failure.

A sporting event, especially for an ardent partisan, often presents a wide spectrum of emotions—joy, sorrow, and a bunch of others in between that mirror the ups and downs of the competition itself, all densely compressed into a single afternoon or evening. But have you ever experienced these emotions, not in a span of a dramatic game or contest or even a rapid sequence but all at once in a sort of explosion, in a way that makes you feel like your soul is expanding?

Five hundred and eighty-six years before the birth of Christ, King Nebuchadnezzar of Babylon leveled the temple in Jerusalem and deported much of the nation to Babylon as slaves. Fifty years later the Persian king, Cyrus, reversed this decision, not only returning the exiles back to Jerusalem but allowing them to rebuild their temple. Then, a little over a year after returning, having obtained fragrant cedar from Lebanon and having selected ideal supervisors for the task, the former exiles were ready to lay the new temple's foundation. Robed priests assembled. Triumphant music swelled. Cymbals and trumpets rang out. Joyous songs were sung. And as they prepared to lay the foundation's first stone, something happened.

Many of the older priests and Levites and family heads, who had seen the former temple, wept aloud when they saw the foundation of this temple being laid (Ezra 3:12). Then, at this climactic moment, the older exiles, having passed from childhood to old age in captivity, were so completely

overcome that suddenly this incredibly sorrow-charged emotion sponta-
neously poured from them all at once in a flurry of tears and sound. No one
could distinguish the shouts of joy from the sound of weeping because the
people made so much noise. And it was heard a long way off (Ezra 3:13).
The Scripture tells us that the overwhelming mixture of emotion produced
such resonant sonic force that it was both heard from far away and remembered for a long, long time. Joy and sorrow flowed together, becoming a
single thing, creating something more powerful than either one alone.

In 1824, Michel Chevreul was working as the director of a factory in
Paris that made tapestries when he began receiving complaints about the
consistency of the colors in the dye of the threads of their products. The
black threads looked one way if adjacent to an orange or a red, that is, a
"hot" color, but then looked quite different next to blue or lavender, a
"cool" color. After a great deal of research and concern, Chevreul realized
there was nothing wrong at the factory. The problem wasn't chemical. *It
was optical.* Assembling all the colors used in the process in slender slices
around a wheel based on their "temperatures," Chevreul found that when
two colors residing on opposite sides of his "color wheel" were laid up
directly against one another, both became more vibrant. For instance, blue
and orange are at opposite sides of the wheel. When he put them right
beside each other, they made each other "pop." Likewise, red brought out
the strong contrast of green. Yellow did so for purple, and so on.[1]

Chevreul's color wheel greatly interested the French Impressionist
painters in the 1800s, including a Post-Impressionist young Dutch artist
named Vincent Van Gogh. Picture in your mind Van Gogh's *Starry Night*—
the spiraling, curving yellows and whites, the thick orange brushstrokes
within his stars and clouds all set against a dark blue sky, the swirling
combination of bold, contrasting colors slammed up right next to each
other, producing actual vibrations in our vision. In this way, Van Gogh
produces a sense of emotional movement in the night air. And the soul
expands to receive it.

Hine Ma Tov is a Jewish hymn traditionally sung at Shabbat feasts. The
lyrics are from Psalm 133: "How good and how pleasant it is that brothers
dwell together." It's an expressive piece in E minor—a pensive, profound,
and "sad" key when played flowingly, delicately. However, then it is set to a
6/8 rhythm—a dancing rhythm, a ballroom rhythm, a "we're all in it here
together" rhythm. The sad E minor key combines with the pleasant lyrics
and more than a hint of bounce to create a feeling akin to a wish, a kind
of longing to be back home together. When at the conclusion of the song

the singers fall into a lilting chorus of "lie, lie, lie" repetitions, the yearning finds consolation. The richness of the song is in the tension of juxtaposed sounds. It expands the soul.

Likewise, when a writer connects language from, in a sense, the opposite sides of the "vocabulary wheel," a similar interesting spark often results. Consider these word combinations: Costly grace. Arresting beauty. Bruised love. Terrific failure. Brilliant regularity. You feel the tension in the adjacent opposites. Something magnetic results in the contrasting emotions, and again the soul expands.

Seasons of difficulty create a backdrop of sadness, even grief, but they also somehow turn up the "poignancy volume" with respect to the adjacent moments of joy that we experience within these seasons. Perhaps we might better pay attention to how these mix together and then hold them up to God as a single thing, receiving the blessing of how they might, in conjunction with one another, expand our souls.

> God, may I tend the juxtapositions and adjacencies of this season, grateful for widening eyes, a higher-capacity heart, and the beauty and light that stand out, not so much against the darkness but with it. May joy and sorrow mix together in memorable ways that can be heard a long way off and remembered with poignancy for a long, long time. Amen.

CHAPTER 59

GOSPEL'D

I was fifteen years old. I was playing catcher for the Cardinals in a summer baseball league. We were contending with our rivals, the Braves. It was the sixth inning and the score was 2 to 2. We had two outs on them and the count was two balls and two strikes to Mike Shannon, their best hitter. We needed just one more strike to get out of the inning, but—and this'll come into play in a moment—they had the go-ahead run on third base. My friend Brock Fairchild was pitching for us, and I called for Brock to throw a curve ball. Brock nodded, took a look at the runner at third, and went into his windup. Mike, expecting the fastball, was fooled and didn't swing, and the ball broke right over the plate. Perfect. Or so I thought. I was so positive, so sure, so certain that it was strike three for the third out that I didn't wait for the umpire's call but pumped my fist, and—thinking the inning was over—just rolled the ball back toward the pitcher's mound and began to head off the field. I was between my third and fourth step toward the dugout when I heard the umpire call not strike three but ball three. *You'll recall now that there was a runner on third base.* Well, now the runner was no longer at third base but was sprinting toward home as the ball was just rolling along on the grass toward Brock on the pitching mound. The runner scored easily and we went on to lose the game 3 to 2.

The moral of this sad tale is this: *Even when you think you're sure you're right, you might leave a little bit of room for the possibility that you're wrong.*

About three years ago, with our younger son, Charlie, Kelly and I went to see our older son, Hank, in a play in Los Angeles. It was called *Titus Andronicus*. The play, as you might know, was written by William Shakespeare in 1593, the first of his eleven tragedies, and, spoiler alert, almost no one gets out of this story alive.

Titus Andronicus, the play's protagonist; Saturninus, the character Hank played; and pretty much everyone else on stage dies by the sword in the show's bloody climactic scene. The play is set in ancient Rome before the time of Christ, and its theme concerns revenge, which is ironic in that no one explores the notion too deeply or hesitates at all in turning to the concept when wronged. There's no real appeal in the play to any other ethic. It is "might makes right" all the way down. And I'm no Shakespeare scholar, but it's a far cry from his later plays *Hamlet* and *Macbeth*.

Macbeth, for instance, is set not in pre-Christian Rome but in eleventh-century Christianized Scotland, and though in the play, Macbeth himself pushes aside his conscience, killing his king and a bevy of others, the Christian ethic remains an obstacle in the path of his ambition all the way through the story. When, for example, Macbeth tries to convince two men to kill his next rival Banquo, claiming that Banquo has wronged both he and the men, the men hesitate and Macbeth responds to them like this: "Do you find patience so predominant in your nature you can let these wrongs go? Are you so *gospel'd* to pray for this man and for his issue...?" (Act 3, sc. 1).

Macbeth is asking himself and the characters before him, as well as us, the audience, a question about Christianity, about the teachings of Christ. He's asking, has the gospel so taken root, so infected all of us, that we can't just take what we want, do what we want, and act as we want without regard to others whom we perceive as in our way? From here forward in the play, the audience begins to see that *Macbeth* is not just about runaway ambition, much as Shakespeare's *Hamlet* is not simply about a guy who can't make up his mind. Shakespeare sets *Macbeth* and *Hamlet* after Christianity's ascendancy, and both give us that lens through which to see issues of revenge.

Though we're not in *Macbeth's* eleventh-century Scotland where we face life-and-death questions concerning in whose hands the government should rest, and we're not in *Hamlet's* fourteenth-century Denmark, called upon to respond with reason to violence and rivalry, and in conscience to family dysfunction, we're still being called upon to respond to Shakespeare's timeless themes and God's eternal questions. The thing is, regardless of the particular conflict at hand, the people involved, or the moment in history, because of Christ, we're always faced with the same tension and the same choice, and it's this: *Will our lives be characterized by power and self-assertion or by sacrificial love, restraint, and a deeply gospel'd humility?*

The gospel calls upon us, no matter our circumstances, to act justly where there is wrong in the world. We're equally called to do the hard work of loving mercy, and walking through our lives and God's world humbly. And just as Macbeth and Hamlet had to decide between ethics, the same question remains for us now. Are we so *gospel'd* that we will refuse to be a part of all the strife and disaffection and contention around us, or will we add to it? Are we so *gospel'd* that we can become a people who are known to answer softly when challenged harshly? Are we so *gospel'd* that we can treat those with whom we disagree with respect and good faith, even when we know it's not likely to be reciprocated? Are we so *gospel'd* that we can internalize the notion that being kind is more important than being right? In a world where people act with so little restraint and with such profound incivility to one another—face to face, online, and behind one another's backs—the question is, *Will we be no different? Or will we be so gospel'd that we will refrain from doing so, and instead love our neighbors as ourselves?*

It all comes down to this: if we've come to believe somehow that it's up to us to withhold grace, to refrain from forgiveness, or to reserve mercy, then maybe, just maybe, we might want to leave a little room for the possibility that we are wrong.

God, I'm in love with being right and seen as being right. It's become a sort of idol for me. Let me better grasp the virtues of humility, patience, and restraint, finding grace even in contention, and letting go of rivalry. Help me, day by day, to be *gospel'd*—to do the hard work of change required to have and maintain the mind of Christ. Amen.

CHAPTER 60

"LOUDER SING FOR EVERY TATTER . . ."

Tom Cole is the director of the McGovern Center for Humanities and Ethics at the UT Health Science Center. He's a Yale grad, holds both a master's and a PhD in history, is a documentary filmmaker, and has written a Pulitzer Prize–nominated book. His latest book is called *Old Man Country: My Search for Meaning among the Elders*, in which he shares a series of deep-dive conversations he's had with twelve distinguished and famous American men, all over eighty years of age. Between the dialogues, Tom splices in vignettes from his own compelling life and sometimes grief-driven work. Tom is a deeply creative soul. In the introduction to his captivating book, he quotes "Sailing to Byzantium" by the Irish poet William Butler Yeats:

> An aged man is but a paltry thing,
> A tattered coat upon a stick, unless
> Soul clap its hands and sing, and louder sing
> For every tatter in its mortal dress.[1]

This season has been a grind not just for the oldest among us but for everyone. At different moments, we seem to be holding on well, and at others we're white-knuckling it. Then, in other moments we feel pretty shredded, leaving us, as Yeats puts it, in tatters, a mere "tattered coat upon a stick." Both Yeats in his poem and Tom in his book tell us that overcoming all that life takes from us requires a soul that claps and sings and, in fact, louder sings for *every tatter* life deals out.

Let's do a little thought exercise: Picture a scale—not a scale you step on to check your weight but the sort you see when you think of the scales of justice, the kind with two plates or bowls suspended at equal distances from a fulcrum. Got it? Now, in your mind's eye, put all the hardships you've faced during this troubled time in one of the plates. What's left you in tatters? Maybe you've lost someone. Maybe you've lost your job. Maybe you're anxious about your health. Maybe you've been picked apart by the vague but exhausting grief of the ongoing loss of experience. Maybe your child was robbed of graduation, prom, or another significant marker of life's passage. Maybe you remain anxious about your young child in a new school or a grown one off to college. Maybe you've not been able to visit a growing grandchild. Whatever it is, put it all over there on one side of the scale.

OK, now what's on the other side? What's going to balance all that out? Or is it just the *kathunk* sound of the heavy side landing on the ground? That's the problem. I think we have to do the imaginative work of placing something over there against all that has ripped up our lives. Both Yeats and Tom Cole suggest that we'll remain tattered unless we find and lean into what makes each of our souls "clap its hands and sing."

For every blow we receive, for every punch we've taken, for every piece of bad news that saps our strength, for every sickness and grief we've absorbed within our aging bodies and spirits, for every tear in our "mortal dress," we must "louder sing."

> An aged man is but a paltry thing
> A tattered coat upon a stick, unless
> Soul clap its hands and sing, and louder sing
> For every tatter in its mortal dress.[2]

What is available and accessible to you now that makes your "soul clap its hands and sing"? Think about it. Do the imaginative work to balance the scales. Here, I'll leave a blank for you: _____.

Go ahead. Fill it in. Whatever it is, let the world hear it from you. Put your thumb on the scale if you have to. You're no paltry thing. No tattered coat upon a stick. From the soul, clap and sing. *Then louder sing!*

> God, the Psalms tell me to clap my hands. The Psalms tell me to shout my God-songs at the top of my lungs. That's especially hard to do right now because I feel so often in tatters. Help me to push back imaginatively against the day with grace but also with strength. Help me to strike back against the season with my faith, knowing that in me, you've made no paltry thing. My soul will clap and sing, and then "louder sing for every tatter in its mortal dress." Amen.

THE LUXURY OF GRACE

When it began, I never imagined that this strange pandemic season would extend so long and then, in effect, give birth to a book about how to get through it. At the time of this writing, we are still wearing masks, still socially distanced from one another, still living under protocols, and still trying to integrate all of this into our lives and into our faith better each day. The organizing theme of this book has been the thought experiment of projecting ourselves forward into the future and asking what we need to be doing now such that, in the future, we might be able to say that we've borne this challenging time well. For me, that's been to try to put my time to use thinking and writing, but I know this has been *a luxury of grace.*

No one in my family or extended family has become seriously ill. My wife and I are both blessed with continued employment, and my kids are navigating the moment well in college and in high school. In the meantime, more than 450,000 Americans have died of COVID-19. Millions have been infected (many with long-term physical and mental-health implications), millions have lost their jobs, and many more are suffering due to social isolation, depression, grief, addiction, financial stress, or poor health due to delayed treatments or undiagnosed problems. I've felt it to be my role to offer hope and encouragement, and I pray that the mostly optimistic tenor of this work does not lead a reader to think that I'm unaware of the tremendous suffering that's occurred and will continue to go on as we find our way out of this trial.

I hear the phrase "there but for the grace of God go I" a good bit, and it rang true to me, mainly when I considered matters such as good health, but, arrogantly, I credited work and conscientiousness as having an outsized part of producing the pleasant life I've lived. I see now that I didn't comprehend the real thrust of this saying about *grace* and *going.*

I see that every good thing in my life is not only grace, not only blessing, not only *not* of my doing but, in some rather distressing sense, just pure luck. Windfall. No one has control of when and where they're born, their DNA, their parents, their lineage, their family, their environment, or much of anything that we think of as markers of success or failure. Further, there are many accidents, momentary failures, betrayals, breaches, and inexplicable glitches in life that can take a person into a serious detour through no real fault of their own. Good people's lives can be easily sidetracked while others somehow generally stay on track such that they continue to prosper or at least get along decently. Grace seems to be a part of it, but this notion implies that grace has been withheld from the less deserving. This notion doesn't make sense to me, nor should it for people who examine matters closely. Is it just luck? That's an unsatisfying conclusion and seems to leave many of the tenets of our faith behind. Is it a combination of a little of this and a little of that? Is it something else? Fate? Who knows?

In the end, all we can do is be grateful for the windfall of life, especially as we begin to see more clearly that we have so little to claim with respect to our own accomplishments, whatever they may be. This awareness, or self-awareness, should summon us toward self-giving and away from self-aggrandizing. As I've noted here, a reasonable measure of self-care makes this more possible. With these three things, *self-awareness, self-care,* and *self-giving,* we craft and curate our lives and then offer them—our DNA, our temperaments, our bodies, our heritage, our luck, our blessing, our education, our work ethic, ourselves—to God to work through us. Perhaps that's it. Perhaps that's everything.

In the end, in this present rough spot in history, that's my prayer here—that God has been made known somehow in the pages of this book, and that through the encouragement embedded in these pages, God will be made known also through you.

— Greg Funderburk, 2021

NOTES

Chapter 2

1. "Few Know How to Enter; Fewer Finish," *New York Times*, March 27, 2013, B-14.

Chapter 3

1. Cited in C. R. Snyder, Shane J. Lopez, and Jennifer Teramoto Pendrotti, *Positive Psychology: The Scientific and Practical Exploration of Human Strengths*, 2nd ed. (Thousand Oaks, CA: Sage Publications, 2011), 244.

Chapter 4

1. David McCullough, "David McCullough on 9/11," National Endowment for the Humanities, excerpted from "First Principles," the Nebraska Governor's Lecture in the Humanities delivered by the author on September 20, 2001, neh.gov/news/david-mccollough-911.

2. Pogosyan, "The Beauty of Imperfection: The Japanese concept of wabi-sabi," January 2, 2017, psychologytoday.com/intl/blog/ between-cultures/201701/the-beauty-imperfection?amp.

3. Byrne, *How Music Works* (San Francisco: McSweeney's, 2012), 44.

4. Pogosyan, "The Beauty of Imperfection."

Chapter 5

1. New York: Charles Scribner's Sons, 1999.

2. Rick Lyman, "Watching Movies with/Ang Lee; Crouching Memory, Hidden Heart," *New York Times*, March 9, 2001, E-1.

3. Lianne Hart and Anne Meier, "The Epic Rescue of Jessica McClure," *People* (November 2, 1987). Available online: people.com/ archive/cover-story-the-epic-rescue-of-jessica-mcclure-vol-28-no-18/.

4. Ibid.

5. Lucy Brock-Broido, "Jessica from the Well," *Virginia Quarterly* 64/3 (Summer 1988); full text available at vqronline.org/jessica-well.

Chapter 6

1. Wiegel, *Witness to Hope* (1999; New York: Harper Perennial, 2004).

Chapter 8

1. See Theater of War Productions at theaterofwar.com as well as Bryan Doerries's memoir, *The Theater of War: What Ancient Greek Tragedies Can Teach Us Today* (New York: Alfred A. Knopf, 2015), and James Shapiro, "'The Theater of War,' by Bryan Doerries," *New York Times* (*Sunday Book Review*), October 2, 2015, p. 21.

2. See Bryan Doerries, trans., *All That You've Seen Here Is God: New Versions of Four Greek Tragedies Sophocles' Ajax, Philoctetes, Women of Trachis; Aeschylus' Prometheus Bound* (New York: First Vintage Books, 2015).

Chapter 9

1. New York: Alfred A. Knopf, 2014.

Chapter 10

1. In Anthony and Ben Holden, eds., *Poems that Make Grown Men Cry* (New York: Simon & Schuster, 2014). Originally published in the *New Yorker* (October 25, 1976): 158. Reprinted with the kind permission of the poet's family.

Chapter 11

1. See Sam Harris, "Q&A with Sam," on wakingup.com; "Don't Meditate Because It's Good for You," dynamic.wakingup.com/player/764c26.

2. *Between God and Man: An Interpretation of Judaism* (New York: Free Press, 1997), 217.

3. Ibid., 218; Heschel, *The Sabbath: Its Meaning for Modern Man* (New York: Farrar, Straus, and Giroux, 2005), 115.

Chapter 12

1. Remy Charlip, *Fortunately* (New York: Simon & Schuster, 1964).

Chapter 14

1. Vincent van Gogh to Theo van Gogh, "on or about" June 28, 1888, Vincent van Gogh Museum, Vincent van Gogh: The Letters (vangoghletters.org/vg/letters/let634/letter.html).

2. Lauren Soth, "Van Gogh's Agony," *Art Bulletin* 68/2 (1986): 307.

Chapter 17

1. San Francisco: Jossey-Bass, 2003.

Chapter 18

1. Peterson, "Prayer and the Practice of Resurrection," 2010 Kistemaker Academic Lecture Series at the Reformed Theological Seminary, Orlando Campus (at available on podcasts.apple.com/us/podcast/prayer-and-the-practice-of-resurrection/id391762172; about minute 34:00–35:00).

2. Ibid., about minute 34:00–35:00.

3. Peterson, *The Contemplative Pastor: Returning to the Art of Spiritual Direction* (Carol Stream, IL: Christianity Today, Inc./Word, Inc., 1989), 120.

Chapter 20

1. "Episode 58: Wilco, 'Magnetized,'" Song Exploder podcast, December 2, 2015.

2. "About Zat Rana," *Medium* (medium.com/@ztrana/about).

3. Zat Rana, "The Most Important Skill Nobody Taught You," *Medium,* June 15, 2018 (medium.com/personal-growth/the-most-important-skill-nobody-taught-you-9b162377ab77).

Chapter 21

1. *Apollo 13*, dir. Ron Howard, screenplay by William Broyles Jr. and Al Reinert, Universal Pictures, June 1995.

Chapter 22

1. Molly Colvin, "That 'Brain Fog' You're Feeling Is Perfectly Normal," WBUR, April 22, 2020 (wbur.org/cognoscenti/2020/04/22/cognitive-change-stress-coronavirus-molly-colvin).

Chapter 23

1. U2, *All That You Can't Leave Behind,* 2000.

Chapter 24

1. U2, "Where the Streets Have No Name," *The Joshua Tree,* 1987.

Chapter 25

1. Guy Winch, "How to Practice Emotional First Aid," TEDxLinnaeusUniversity (youtube.com/watch?v=rni41c9iq54; about minute 11:00–12:30); see also Guy Winch, *Emotional First Aid* (New York: Hudson Street Press, 2013).

2. "Ending Poverty," un.org/en/sections/issues-depth/poverty/.

3. "Understanding Poverty," worldbank.org/en/understanding-poverty (accessed December 10, 2020).

4. UNESCO Institute for Statistics, "Literacy Rates Continue to Rise from One Generation to the Next," (uis.unesco.org/sites/default/files/documents/fs45-literacy-rates-continue-rise-generation-to-next-en-2017_0.pdf).

5. Drew Desilver, "Despite global concerns about democracy, more than half of countries are democratic," May 14, 2019, Pew Research Center (pewresearch.org/fact-tank/2019/05/14/more-than-half-of-countries-are-democratic/).

6. Pew Research Center, "The Future of World Religions: Population Growth Projections, 2010–2050," April 2, 2015 (pewforum.org/2015/04/02/religious-projections-2010-2050/).

Chapter 27

1. Peterson, *Contemplative Pastor*, 33–34.

Chapter 28

1. Tobolowsky, *My Adventures with God* (New York: Simon and Schuster, 2017), 175–84.

Chapter 29

1. Cain, *Quiet* (New York: Broadway Books, 2012), 81–83.

Chapter 30

1. Andrea Peer, "Global poverty: Facts, FAQs, and How to Help," October 16, 2020, World Vision (worldvision.org/sponsorship-news-stories/global-poverty-facts).

2. UNICEF, "Under Five Mortality," September 2020 (data.unicef.org/topic/child-survival/under-five-mortality/).

3. *Middlemarch* (New York: Bantam, 1992), 766.

Chapter 31

1. Lamott, "12 Truths I Learned from Life and Writing," TED2017 (April) (www.ted.com/talks/anne_lamott_12_truths_i_learned_from_life_and_writing?language=en).

2. Kahn, *The Boys of Summer* (New York: Harper & Row, 1987), 293.

3. Craddock, *Luke* (Int; Louisville: Westminster/John Knox Press, 2009), 72.

Chapter 32

1. *Søren Kierkegaard's Journals and Papers*, vol. 5 (Bloomington: Indiana University Press, 1978), 412.

Chapter 33

1. Saul McLeod, "Solomon Asch—Conformity Experiment," December 28, 2018, SimplyPsychology.org (simplypsychology.org/asch-conformity.html).

2. Wiman, *My Bright Abyss: Meditation of a Modern Believer* (New York: Farrar, Straus, and Giroux, 2013), 121.

Chapter 34

1. James, *The Varieties of Religious Experience* (London: Longmans, Green, 1902), 204.

Chapter 36

1. For a helpful summary of the study, see Peter A Noone, "The Holmes-Rahe Stress Inventory," *Occupational Medicine* 67/7 (October 2017): 581–82 (doi.org/10.1093/occmed/kqx099).

2. See American Institute of Stress, "The Holmes-Rahe Stress Inventory," stress.org/holmes-rahe-stress-inventory.

3. Heschel, *I Asked for Wonder: A Spiritual Anthology* (New York: Crossroad, 2004), 34–35.

4. Heschel, *The Sabbath*, 13.

5. "How Sleep Clears the Brain," NIH Research Matters, October 28, 2013, National Institutes of Health (nih.gov/news-events/nih-research-matters/how-sleep-clears-brain).

6. Steinbeck, *Sweet Thursday* (1954; New York: Penguin, 2008), 107.

Chapter 38

1. "The Skyscraper," *Digital History* (digitalhistory.uh.edu/disp_textbook.cfm?smtid=2&psid=3050).

Chapter 40

1. New York: Crown, 2015.

2. Directed and screenplay by Steven Zaillian, Paramount Pictures, 1993.

3. Robert Sobel, *Coolidge: An American Enigma* (Washington, DC: Regnery Pub., 1998), 242.

Chapter 41

1. Interestingly, about 75 percent of respondents in both the non-drug and psychedelics groups rated their "God encounter" experience as among the most meaningful and spiritually significant in their lifetime. Further, independent of psychedelics use, more than two-thirds of those who said they were atheists before the experience no longer identified as such afterward.

2. Johns Hopkins Medicine Newsroom, "Experiences of 'Ultimate Reality' or 'God' Confer Lasting Benefits to Mental Health," April 23, 2019 (hopkinsmedicine.org/news/newsroom/news-releases/experiences-of-ultimate-reality-or-god-confer-lasting-benefits-to-mental-health); Roland R. Griffiths, et al., "Survey of subjective 'God encounter experiences': Comparisons among naturally occurring experiences and those occasioned by the classic psychedelics psilocybin, LSD, ayahuasca, or DMT," *PLoS ONE* 14/4 (April 2019): e0214377 (https://doi.org/10.1371/journal.pone.0214377).

3. New York: Seven Stories Press, 2013.

4. From "Advice to Graduating Women (That All Men Should Know)," commencement address to Agnes Scott College, Decatur, Georgia, May 15, 1999, in *If This Isn't Nice, What Is?* (New York: Seven Stories Press, 2013).

Chapter 43

1. Reprinted with permission of Harvard University Press from *The Poems of Emily Dickinson: Variorum Edition*, edited by Ralph W. Franklin, Cambridge, Mass.: The Belknap Press of Harvard University Press, Copyright © 1998 by the President and Fellows of Harvard College. Copyright © 1951, 1955 by the President and Fellows of Harvard College. Copyright © renewed 1979, 1983 by the President and Fellows of Harvard College. Copyright © 1914, 1918, 1919, 1924, 1929, 1930, 1932, 1935, 1937, 1942 by Martha Dickinson Bianchi. Copyright © 1952, 1957, 1958, 1963, 1965 by Mary L. Hampson.

2. Brooks, *Love Your Enemies* (New York: Broadside Books, 2019), 189.

Chapter 45

1. *One Step Closer* (Grand Rapids: Brazos Press, 2006), 111–12.